Some Like It Hot

Some Like It Hot

PLANTS THAT THRIVE IN HOT AND HUMID WEATHER

P.J. GARTIN and F. BRIAN SMITH

WYRICK & COMPANY

Published by Wyrick & Company
Post Office Box 89
Charleston, SC 29402

Designed by Sally Heineman

Printed and bound in Canada

Library of Congress Cataloging-in-Publication Data

ISBN 0-941711-74-9

Contents

Acknowledgements

When we began writing *Some Like It Hot*, we never anticipated the unwavering support we received from so many. We would like to thank Jack Bernens, Susan Day, Marcia Miles, and Paul Thompson for their willingness to share their superb editing skills with us. We are also grateful to Paul for giving us his magnificent chart on Crepe Myrtle characteristics and for reading *Some Like It Hot* with the critical eye of an expert horticulturist. We also thank the National Arboretum's Dr. Margaret Pooler for her breeding data on Crepe Myrtles, as well as information on the late Dr. Don Egolf's research. We are likewise indebted to the staff at the Charleston Library Society, The Citadel's Daniel Library, and the Charleston County Public Library. No question or request was ever considered trivial and we owe them our deepest gratitude.

We are also beholden to our amazing photographer, Vin Duffy, who unselfishly gave up a perfect lowcountry Sunday afternoon for our author photo shoot at Magnolia Gardens. And we wish to thank Magnolia Gardens director Taylor Nelson, as well as the rest of the staff, for allowing us unfettered access to this fascinating historic property.

We are obliged to American Horticultural Society President Emeritus Dr. Marc Cathey. His creation of the AHS Plant Heat-Zone map has been a wonderful gift to all gardeners and his recent collaboration with the U.S. Department of Agriculture to update their cold-hardiness map makes plant selection much simpler for all of us. We also acknowledge Thompson & Morgan for sharing their very reliable seed-raising information.

Of course, our most heartfelt thanks goes to our spouses, Amy Smith and Jack Bernens, for their unfailing support, patience, and kindness. We are forever grateful to our publishers, Pete and Connie Wyrick, for giving us the opportunity to realize our stubborn conviction that there really was a book in us. We are also indebted to our kind and patient editor, Laura Moses, and to our very talented book designer, Sally Heineman. And finally, we wish to thank our departed friend and fellow gardener Beverly Colman for inspiring us to travel beyond mundane destinations.

Introduction

If you picked up this book expecting a steamy guide to improving your love life, or a culinary exposé about hot peppers, we didn't intend to mislead you. *Some Like It Hot* is a gardening guide about how to select and grow landscape plants that will not only survive, but also thrive, in summer's heat and humidity.

Zebrinus Maidenhair
Grass
Miscanthus sinensis
'Zebrinus'

As an Extension Service County Agent (Brian) and a Master Gardener (P.J.), we have more than twenty years of southern gardening experience between us. We know first hand the frustration and confusion of figuring out what kinds of plants will give our gardens ornamental value during the heat of summer. And like everyone else who lives south of the thirty-ninth parallel (39N), and is affected by weather brought up by the Gulf of Mexico, we have encountered the horticultural joys and disappointments of growing plants during subtropical southeastern summers. Both of us can conjure up a few good horticultural horror stories that would send most "snowbirds"—a southern designation for northerners who stay with us only during the winter, then flee once temperatures begin to rise past eighty degrees—packing by early February.

But we also know that a substantial number of snowbirds eventually make Dixie their permanent home. (Welcome, y'all.) So, we wrote *Some Like It Hot* not only for veteran deep south gardeners who are always willing to expand their horticultural horizons, but also for the inexperienced, just-moved-here-from-the-north novice. *Some Like It Hot* is also an invaluable guide for the already knowledgeable southern gardener who has moved into another USDA Hardiness Zone. Just moving from Zone 7a to 8b can be a perplexing horticultural experience! It's usually difficult to reset our botanical clocks without some assistance.

Although thousands of words have been written about plants that will survive heat, many "sure-fire formulas" turn out to be horticultural disappointments. Suggested plants are often not available from local garden centers or, after you've read about a perfect plant for a troublesome spot in your garden, it's too late in the season to start it from seed. Of course, the ultimate nightmare is carefully following growing instructions only to have the plants wilt and die in the middle of summer, when it's botanically impossible to start over again. Plants that fall short of our expectations also frustrate commercial growers and retailers. Failure to offer gardeners heat-tolerant plants is a missed sales opportunity.

We believe that a successful gardener should understand the physiology of plants and soils before depending on a plant classification system or a list of plants. That's why *Some Like It Hot* is more than just a compendium of landscape plants that will tolerate heat and high humidity. And while the horticulturist and home gardener both rely on the American Horticulture Society's (AHS) Heat Zones, as well as the USDA's Hardiness Zones, it's been our experience that these resources are not answers in themselves.

One of the challenges to learning about heat-tolerant plants is a matter of adjusting our perceptions. As horticultural experts and deep south gardeners, we know all too well that "hot weather" is a relative term. Although it's true that geographical regions share common climatic conditions, within each region are varied degrees of heat. Take the Carolinas as an example. In the foothills of Spartanburg County, South Carolina, which is one hour away from Asheville, North Carolina, "hot" for a Spartanburg gardener is 95° F with 75% humidity during the day, and around 70° F at night. Yet, Asheville is much cooler than Spartanburg in the summer. Asheville is 2,250 feet above sea level and the city of Spartanburg is at 875 feet. Botanically speaking, every 1,000 feet in elevation is the same as moving up 600 miles in latitude.

Head southeast from Spartanburg a mere 200 miles to Charleston, South Carolina, and those same weather conditions are considered just "very warm." Hot for Charleston is 98° F with 95% humidity during the day and 80° F at night. If that doesn't seem like much of a climatic difference, just come visit Charleston in August! In other words, some plants that survive Spartanburg's heat melt away to oblivion in Charleston.

Natchez Crepe
Myrtle
Lagerstroemia
'Natchez'

About This Book

The goal of this book is quite simple. We will show you how to find and to use plants that like hot and humid weather. We all know that cacti and other desert plants like hot, dry weather; however, they do not like humid conditions. In the hot, dry desert, the humidity is very low or almost nonexistent. Most of the United States has hot, humid conditions in the summer, even during droughts. Desert plants transplanted to the humid east coast will falter under the pressure of humidity unless they're potted indoors where the relative humidity is much lower.

It should be fairly obvious that plants native to high-humidity regions are most likely to survive in American southeastern gardens. However, in addition to identifying the kinds of plants that like hot, humid conditions, we must also select the ones that can survive without regular rainfall or in drought conditions. We could look to the equatorial rainforest, but then the problem of cold-hardiness becomes an issue. Are you throwing up your hands, wondering what to do? The answer is often in your backyard or, more accurately, in the woods behind your backyard.

White Beautyberry
Callicarpa dichotoma albifructus

We should always look to native flora first because they should be the backbone of any hot weather landscape. However, the options from our native flora often are not enough for most gardeners. So we turn east—Far East, that is. The best place to look for other plants that will do well in our hot, humid weather is to look at the native plants of other parts of the world with the same hot, humid weather as ours. If you've ever wondered why 3,000 Yoshino cherry trees (*Prunus × yedoensis*), native to Japan, thrive around Washington, DC's Tidal Basin, it's because Washington and Tokyo share similar climatic conditions. Washington, DC is at 38.53 N and Tokyo is 35.42 N.

Southern China is another example. The city of Shanghai is about on the same latitude as Charleston (Charleston is at 32.46 N and Shanghai is 31.14 N).

Haul out a world atlas and look at all the places in the world that are on the same imaginary line that divides north and south. If you conduct the exer-

Chickasaw
Crepe Myrtle
Lagerstroemia ×
fauriei 'Chickasaw'

cise for Charleston, you will find that Los Angeles is on about the same latitude. In case you are not well informed about the gardening climates in Los Angeles and Charleston, they're not very much alike! Los Angeles has a more moderate temperature range and less humidity than Charleston. You'll need to do a little detective work here. Latitude is just part of the picture. There's more to this geography lesson. Let's look more closely at Charleston, Los Angeles, and Shanghai.

Charleston and Shanghai are seaport cities. Both have the ocean to their east and land to their west. Los Angeles is a seaport city too. However, the ocean is to its *west* and the land to its *east*. The ocean currents run closer to the coast of California than they do to the coasts of South Carolina and China. Consequently, the climate of Shanghai is more like Charleston's than is that of Los Angeles.

Now you understand why the first question asked by an experienced plantsperson is "Where does it come from?" If someone says a particular shrub

Small Anise-Tree
Illicium parviflorum

is native to the Mediterranean, we know it will like our southeastern temperatures, but it might have a problem surviving the humidity. If, however, we're told that same plant is from the south China Sea region near Hong Kong, we probably have a winner, if it's not too cold-sensitive. In either case, we would have to carefully monitor its growth to see how it responds to our climate.

A plant shouldn't be dismissed just because it doesn't experience high humidity in its native habitat. It just means that if it's going to falter, humidity will be the likely culprit. Plants not adapted to muggy conditions may not be resistant to the diseases that are prevalent in high humidity. They just don't have tough enough skin to repel disease when high humidity gives the fungus or bacteria the advantage in the infection battle.

How to Use This Book

Everyone wants landscape plants that offer ornamental value during the hot summer months. However, we all know there's nothing more vexing that having to fuss over heat-stressed plants when it's still 86° at dusk and the mosquitoes are relentless. So, in addition to having low summertime maintenance and excellent durability, our criteria for *Some Like It Hot* plants is that they must offer robust bloom, vibrant berries, interesting bark, or, at the very least, display exceptional leaf color. This does not mean, however, that our selections are exclusive. Other plants survive deep south summers and they are listed in the last chapter.

We know very few people who have ever sat down and *completely* read a gardening book from cover to cover. Gardeners often need quick answers, so we've included easy to use "At-a-Glance" lists, including one that categorizes plants by color. *Some Like It Hot* may also be used as a reference book to look up a specific plant's native habitat and mature height, as well as its AHS Heat Zone and UDSA Hardiness Zone rating. You can also use it as a general gardening book to help you plan your landscape for heat- and humidity-loving plants.

If you are unfamiliar with the AHS Heat Zone Map, please read our explanation on how to interpret this invaluable tool. We're sure that the more you use our book, the more confident you'll become in recognizing the characteristics of a *Some Like It Hot* plant.

How to Get the Most out of the Plant Hardiness and Heat Zone Maps

For more than thirty years, gardeners have consulted the U.S. Department of Agriculture (USDA) Plant Hardiness Zones before deciding to invest time and money on a particular landscape plant. That's because the Hardiness Zones are fairly accurate predictors of a plant's survivability in a given geographical area. However, a lot of southern gardeners have added a peculiar twist to the Hardiness Zone interpretations. It goes something like this: Although each zone is defined as the average annual minimum temperature for a particular area, we also know that "hardiness" implies a year-round capability to survive. A lot of deep south gardeners figure that a plant's chances for summer survival

Leatherleaf Mahonia
Mahonia bealei

might increase if it was recommended for the next higher zone. For example, if a particular plant was rated hardy in Zone 9, but not listed for Zone 8, then folks gardening along the Carolina coast and much of the Florida coastline assume the plant would survive the summer heat because it could grow in an even hotter climate. The problem, of course, is that even the balmiest of southern winters can turn dreadfully cold, so everyone ends up playing a horticultural version of Russian roulette with his or her not-so-cold-hardy plants.

It's important to remember that the average annual minimum temperatures for each of the eleven USDA Hardiness Zones increase in increments of 10°F. Zone 9's average annual minimum temperatures are from 20°–30°F. Zone 8 drops to 10°–20°F. In many cases, even a two-degree drop in temperature can kill a subtropical plant. In some ways that's a blessing when it comes to a plant's cold tolerance. Once it freezes, it's toast. The chances for a miraculous recovery are slim.

Heat-related deaths aren't always easy to recognize. The plant's overall health may decline slowly, taking several years before it dies. (In the meantime, you're pulling your hair out, wondering what's wrong with your plant, messing with the pH, wasting inordinate amounts of fertilizer, and spraying with abandon.)

In the late nineties, American Horticultural Society President Emeritus Marc Cathey created the Heat-Zone Map. Based on the fact that plants begin a physiological decline at temperatures over 86°F, his map's zones are segmented into the average number of "heat days." Zone 12, which is the hottest, has an average of 210 days above 86°, while Zone 1 has less than one.

Although the Heat-Zone Map uses twelve zones instead of the USDA's eleven, the concepts are quite compatible and extremely useful. Use the Heat-Zone Map exactly as you use the USDA Plant Hardiness Zone Map. The USDA's map determines cold hardiness, while the American Horticultural Society's Heat-Zone Map measures heat hardiness. When used in tandem, they become powerful tools.

The following example shows how to use both tables before selecting a plant for your garden.

One of the most popular summer-blooming shrubs in southern gardens is the Mophead version of the Bigleaf Hydrangea, *H. macrophylla* subsp. *macrophylla*. It's noted for its big, round flower clusters, which is probably why a lot of northerners call white hydrangeas "Snowballs." However, many deep south gardeners have probably never seen a snow-white Mophead. Our flowers are usually pink or blue, depending on the pH of our naturally acidic soil. However, the variation and intensity of color is actually triggered by the availability of aluminum. It's more abundant in soils with low pH. *H. macrophylla* subsp. *macrophylla* is rated in Hardiness Zones 6 through 9. Geographically,

that's from about Cincinnati, Ohio, to considerably south of Tampa Bay in Florida. The American Horticultural Society's Heat-Zone rating for Mopheads is 3 through 9. Now the classification changes dramatically to include spotty areas near the Canadian border and high mountain places, and just past southern Georgia into northern Florida.

Lacecap Hydrangea
Hydrangea macrophylla normalis

USDA Plant Hardiness Zone Map

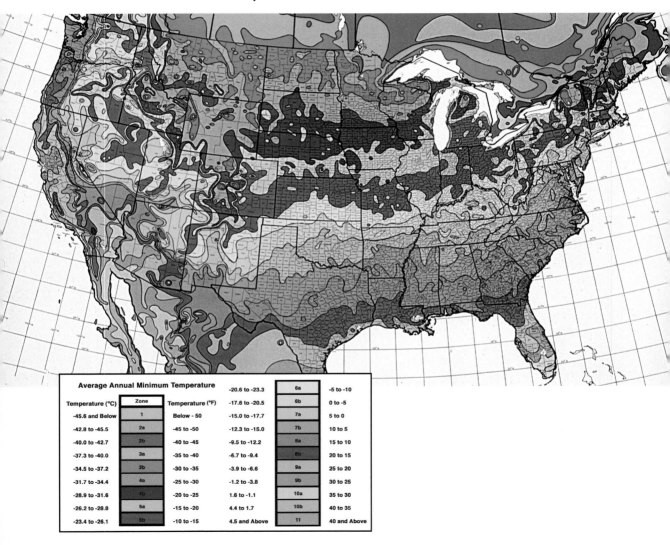

Average Annual Minimum Temperature					
Temperature (°C)	Zone	Temperature (°F)	-20.6 to -23.3	6a	-5 to -10
-45.6 and Below	1	Below -50	-17.6 to -20.5	6b	0 to -5
-42.8 to -45.5	2a	-45 to -50	-15.0 to -17.7	7a	5 to 0
-40.0 to -42.7	2b	-40 to -45	-12.3 to -15.0	7b	10 to 5
-37.3 to -40.0	3a	-35 to -40	-9.5 to -12.2	8a	15 to 10
-34.5 to -37.2	3b	-30 to -35	-6.7 to -9.4	8b	20 to 15
-31.7 to -34.4	4a	-25 to -30	-3.9 to -6.6	9a	25 to 20
-28.9 to -31.6	4b	-20 to -25	-1.2 to -3.8	9b	30 to 25
-26.2 to -28.8	5a	-15 to -20	1.6 to -1.1	10a	35 to 30
-23.4 to -26.1	5b	-10 to -15	4.4 to 1.7	10b	40 to 35
			4.5 and Above	11	40 and Above

Let's assume that we live in Charleston, South Carolina, which is in USDA Plant Hardiness Zone 8b and AHS Plant Heat-Zone 8. According to the charts, Hardiness Zone 8 has average annual minimum temperatures of 10° to 20° F and Heat-Zone 8 has more than 90 days over 86° F, but fewer than 121. Taking both ratings into consideration, and with some common sense gardening practices, *H. macrophylla* subsp. *macrophylla* should survive our hot, humid summers and also make it through the winter.

[Note: It's never safe to assume that Hardiness Zone ratings and Heat-Zone ratings will always be the same. It just turns out that a lot of places share the same number. Although much of the deep south is in Hardiness Zone 8, some areas are in Heat-Zone 9, as well as Heat-Zone 8.]

Jack Bernens remembers the hydrangea that grew in his mother's Price Hill garden in Cincinnati. Everyone called it a Snowball. It was a big, white, early-summer bloomer that produced huge, floppy flower heads. He thought it was magnificent.

However, his mother's hydrangea most likely wasn't a Mophead. *Hydrangea arborescens* is a native that grows in USDA Hardiness Zones 3–9. Sometimes called wild or smooth hydrangea, the plant Jack recalls was probably the midwestern variety called 'Grandiflora' or 'Hills of Snow'. It was discovered growing wild in Ohio during the early 1900s. From what we can gather, it never gained widespread popularity because of its propensity to grow to almost unmanageable proportions, and because its large, robust flowers usually sagged. Although hardly the kind of plant for those who demand a carefully coiffed landscape, we have read that they are truly spectacular.

Another variety named 'Annabelle', which originally hailed from Illinois, became a hydrangea of note during the same period. Slightly better behaved than her Buckeye cousin, she prefers moist, organically-rich soil and partial shade. The chartreuse-green flower heads appear in midsummer and then mature to a velvety cream color by autumn.

American Horticultural Society Plant Heat-Zone Map

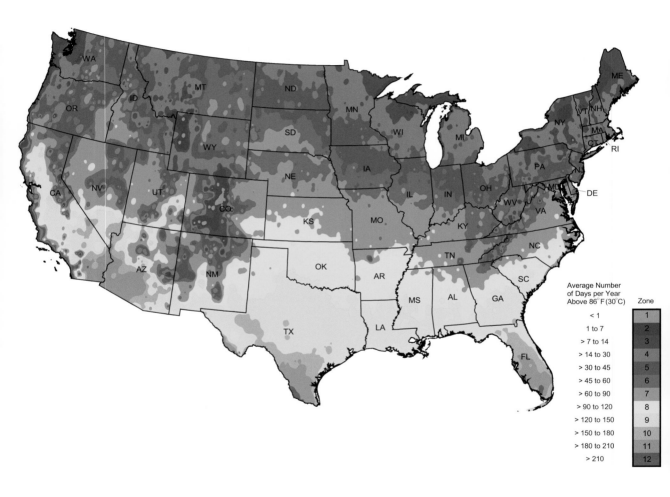

Average Number of Days per Year Above 86°F (30°C)	Zone
< 1	1
1 to 7	2
> 7 to 14	3
> 14 to 30	4
> 30 to 45	5
> 45 to 60	6
> 60 to 90	7
> 90 to 120	8
> 120 to 150	9
> 150 to 180	10
> 180 to 210	11
> 210	12

Reproduced with permission of the American Horticultural Society

Average Relative Humidity, Elevation, and Longitude of Major Southern Cities

City	Annual Average Relative Humidity Morning/Evening	July and August Average Relative Humidity Morning/Evening	Elevation	Longitude and Latitude
Birmingham, AL	84/60%	July: 86/61% – Aug: 87/60%	600 ft.	33.31 N – 86.48 W
Mobile, AL	87/62%	July: 90/65% – Aug: 91/65%	5 ft.	30.41 N – 88.02 W
Montgomery, AL	86/60%	July: 90/63% – Aug: 91/63%	160 ft.	32.33 N – 86.18 W
Little Rock, AR	83/59%	July: 86/58% – Aug: 85/57%	286 ft.	34.44 N – 92.17 W
Jacksonville, FL	89/56%	July: 89/59% – Aug: 91/61%	20 ft.	30.19 N – 81.39 W
Tallahassee, FL	90/55%	July: 94/61% – Aug: 95/61%	150 ft.	30.26 N – 84.16 W
Atlanta, GA	82/56%	July: 88/59% – Aug: 89/60%	1050 ft.	33.44 N – 82.43 W
Savannah, GA	86/54%	July: 89/57% – Aug: 91/60%	20 ft.	32.05 N – 81.06 W
Baton Rouge, LA	89/63%	July: 92/66% – Aug: 92/65%	57 ft.	30.27 N – 91.09 W
New Orleans, LA	87/65%	July: 91/68% – Aug: 91/68%	5 ft.	29.57 N – 90.04 W
Jackson, MS	90/61%	July: 93/63% – Aug: 94/62%	940 ft.	32.17 N – 90.11 W
Asheville, NC	90/57%	July: 95/62% – Aug: 97/63%	1985 ft.	35.36 N – 82.33 W
Raleigh, NC	85/54%	July: 89/58% – Aug: 92/59%	365 ft.	35.46 N – 78.38 W
Charleston, SC	86/56%	July: 88/62% – Aug: 90/63%	9 ft.	32.46 N – 79.55 W
Chattanooga, TN	86/56%	July: 89/57% – Aug: 91/57%	675 ft.	35.02 N – 85.81 W
Galveston, TX	83/72%	July: 81/70% – Aug: 81/69%	5 ft.	29.17 N – 94.47 W
Houston, TX	90/64%	July: 92/62% – Aug: 92/62%	40 ft.	29.45 N – 95.21 W
Norfolk, VA	78/52%	July: 81/59% – Aug: 84/62%	10 ft.	36.50 N – 76.17 W
Richmond, VA	83/53%	July: 85/56% – Aug: 89/57%	160 ft.	37.33 N – 77.27 W

Ornamental Grasses

Ornamental grasses can add many things to our gardens that other plants cannot. Their most significant aspect in the landscape is not color (because we can get color from lots of other sources), but *texture*.

No other kinds of plants can offer us such fine, soft texture as ornamental grasses. For example, Purple Fountain Grass (*Pennisetum setaceum* 'Rubrum') in full bloom, with the sun behind it, is soft and translucent. Add a slight breeze, and motion has joined the aesthetic palette. The soft edges of the flower/seed heads, and the blades dancing back and forth in the breeze, are reminiscent of lapping ocean waves. Watching this can be almost as soothing and satisfying as sitting on the beach. When you realize that you're still in your front yard, it just goes to show what an awesome impact ornamental grasses can have on the landscape.

Purple Fountain Grass
Pennisetum setaceum
'Rubrum'

Ornamental grasses have many benefits. Not only are they one of the best sources of texture for our landscapes, they can soften harsh transitions. A bed of medium to tall ornamental grass works great to downplay a sharp corner view of a building. With their rapid growth rate, ornamental grasses can be used to hide unsightly objects. Another benefit of ornamental grasses that is often overlooked, and will become increasingly important as gardeners strive to do their part in natural resource conservation, is their ability to quickly cover an area and hold the soil in place to reduce erosion. Ornamental grasses, when used judiciously, can be great buffer/transition zone plants along waterway banks and pond edges. The area immediately adjacent to a body of water must have plant material to stabilize the soil and act as a filter to reduce pollutants entering the water.

Ornamental grasses are also an important component of wildlife management. The grassy clumps can provide a place of cover for many animals and make good nesting sites for birds.

Most people think of the ubiquitous—and grossly overused—pampas grass or liriope when ornamental grasses are mentioned. If you are one of those gardeners who have experienced the unfortunate fate of not being introduced to the rest of the ornamental grass world, then the next several pages are going to be a plethora of delight and excitement. You will leave this chapter with a new appreciation for the great benefits that ornamental grasses can bring to your garden.

Bushy Bluestem

Andropogon glomeratus

Native to the eastern coastal U.S., this grass is well known by coastal plains residents for its proliferation in wet areas. As its native habitat suggests, this grass thrives on moisture, but it makes an excellent ornamental grass for any type of garden—provided you keep it well watered. You don't need to create a marshland or wetland to grow this plant. Just make sure it gets regular watering, especially during a drought. While Bushy Bluestem does offer color and texture during the summer, its fall color is most significant. Its autumn bronze color alerts even the casual passerby that winter is not far off. The benefits don't end with its foliage color, though. Just as the foliage starts to change color in the late summer, it produces soft, fluffy, off-white flower heads at the end of each stem.

Some Like It Hot **Ornamental Grasses**

Andropogon glomeratus	Bushy Bluestem
Calamagrostis brachytricha	Korean Feather Reed Grass
Carex spp.	Sedge
Chasmanthium latifolium	Wild Oats, Upland Sea Oats
Cortaderia selloana	Pampas Grass
Cymbopogon citratus	Lemon Grass
Imperata cylindrica 'Rubra'	Japanese Blood Grass
Liriope spp.	Liriope, Monkey Grass, Lilyturf
L. muscari 'Big Blue'	Big Blue Liriope
L. spicata	Creeping Lilyturf
L. grandiflora	Evergreen Giant Liriope
Miscanthus spp.	Miscanthus, Maidenhair Grass
Muhlenbergia capillaris	Sweetgrass, Pink Muhly
M. filipes	Sweetgrass, Purple Muhly
Ophiopogon japonicus	Mondo Grass
O. japonicus 'Nana'	Dwarf Mondo Grass
Panicum virgatum	Panic Grass, Switch-Grass
Pennisetum alopecuroides	Fountain Grass
P. setaceum 'Rubrum' formerly *P. alopecuroides* 'Rubrum'	Purple Fountain Grass

While small clumps placed in the correct spot can accent your landscape, a massive planting of Bushy Bluestem in a large area may be its best use for your garden.

Bushy Bluestem grows to a height of 2–4 feet depending on solar exposure. It will establish itself in either sand or clay, provided it gets enough moisture. It is the perfect plant for prolonged moist soils that occasionally dry out. In the wild, it is most often seen in the transition zone between the upland and the wetland.

Height: 2–4 feet • Spread: clumps 1–2 feet wide • Sun: full to light shade • Moisture: regular moisture, especially during a drought • Hardiness Zone: 5–10 • Heat Zone: 7–11 (estimated) • Propagation: seed or division

Korean Feather Reed Grass
Calamagrostis brachytricha

This clump-forming, upright, arching grass is native to eastern Asia. It is found growing along the edges of woods and moist woodlands in Korea and other east Asian countries. Its ornamental value is in the arching green leaf blades and the purple flowers that form in September. The flowers start purple then fade to a silver gray within a few weeks. The flower parts hold for a long time, which makes them good candidates for dry cut-flower arrangements.

One of the things we like about Korean Feather Reed Grass is its fine texture. During the summer, even the slightest breeze easily moves the thin, new-growth leaf blades. Then, as late summer approaches and the seed heads form, soft blades and fluffy flower heads nod and dance in the breeze. While this plant's visual appeal is versatile enough to use as a specimen or in containers, we prefer to see it planted in masses, creating a sea of waving foliage and flower heads.

From a gardener's point of view, Korean Feather Reed Grass is well behaved and not finicky. While it performs best where some moisture is regularly available, it will survive through drought periods. You can use this grass in sun or shade, but Brian believes it will have better results in shady spots where soil stays a little moist. When you consider that environments like this are often difficult places to establish plants, this grass becomes a real plus. So, if you have such a spot in your yard and don't have a clue what to do with it, try some Korean Feather Reed Grass.

Height: 4 feet • Spread: clumps 1–2 feet wide • Sun: full sun or shade • Moisture: likes a moist soil • Hardiness Zone: 4–9 • Heat Zone: 4–9 (estimated) • Propagation: seed or division

Sedge

Carex spp.

The number of sedge species just in the *Carex* genus is enough to make your head spin. There are more than two thousand of them! And almost every one comes from a moist area somewhere in the world. Therefore, they are excellent choices when you want an ornamental grass but are limited to planting in heavy soil or on a wet site. Most sedges are not grown for their flowers (although some do have them), but for foliage color. You can find sedges in colors ranging from green to blue to orange to bronze, and some are variegated. Brian finds that the bronze-colored species are used more frequently, and their best visual effect comes from contrasting hues and textures.

Sedge clumps are somewhat airy, which adds to their unusual texture. Some stand straight and rigid, while others weep like a willow tree. If used in large numbers, the weeping ones will create a river-like look when planted around other kinds of ornamental grasses. If you are looking for an interesting accent or unusual color, this is the grass to purchase.

One species of *Carex* is worth special attention. Frosty Curls or Blonde Sedge (*Carex albula*) has silvery, almost white, foliage. It's a spectacular sight to see it cascade to the ground. We also like

Sedge
Carex spp.

this plant because of its usefulness on inclined areas and berms. It will produce clumps of very fine silvery blades that arch back to the ground and flow along the contour of the soil surface. This "flowing" aspect also makes outstanding potted plants if the containers are tall enough.

Carex albula grows best in full sun but accepts partial shade. The catch with Frosty Curls is its cold hardiness. It is a USDA Zone 7 plant, native to New Zealand. Plants from there are usually able to take our heat and humidity, but we often find their cold hardiness somewhat lacking. While many deep south gardeners can successfully overwinter this plant, our cooler-zoned friends will have to pay attention to the temperatures.

Wild Oats
Chasmanthium latifolium

Height: a few inches–4 feet • Spread: clumps 1–2 feet wide • Sun: varies with species • Moisture: usually needs regular watering and a moist soil • Hardiness Zone: varies by species • Heat Zone: varies by species • Propagation: seed or division

Wild Oats, Upland Sea Oats
Chasmanthium latifolium

Chasmanthium latifolium is the quintessential southern native grass. Found in moist thickets, creek bottoms and wooded slopes in the southeastern U.S., it ranges from Texas all the way to Pennsylvania and New Jersey. For some reason, this species was originally included in the *Uniola* (sea oats) genus and that is how it acquired its common name, upland sea oats. However, there is nothing maritime about that plant and some plant taxonomists get testy about referring to *C. latifolium* as sea oats.

Wild oats is a visually interesting, multi-purpose plant. With its flat, oat-like seed heads that turn bronze by autumn, it will hold its form and color throughout the winter. Edge a bed with it or plant it by itself in sweeping masses. Wild oats also makes an excellent ground cover, or if you have no room in the landscape, pot one for an accent plant. This plant can also be used in dried flower arrangements.

Wild oats tolerates a wide range of soils and climates, which means that it's very easy to grow. Although it performs best in full sun to part shade, *C. latifolium* will not lose its good looks if planted in the shade. In fact, this is the perfect plant for an area that doesn't receive much sun, with soil that doesn't dry out too quickly. No matter where or how you use wild oats, just make sure that it receives some early morning or late evening sun. That's because the bronze seed heads are showiest when the sun reflects off of them at low angles. This native plant has great landscaping potential and is just waiting for the gardening public to discover it.

Height: 3–4 feet • Spread: clumps 1–2 feet • Sun: full sun or shade • Moisture: needs regular moisture in full sun, tolerates dry soil in shade • Hardiness Zone: 5–10 • Heat Zone: 4–11 (estimated) • Propagation: seeds or division in spring

Wild Oats
Chasmanthium latifolium

Pampas Grass
Cortaderia selloana

Ugh, a plant that has been so overused that we cringe at the name! Why is it that some plants become universally accepted, while others never get noticed? If it weren't so grossly overused, we'd be big pampas grass fans. That's because pampas grass *does* have great qualities. It tolerates everything our climate can throw at it. The stuff grows without any attention paid to it, and it produces big, very attractive flower heads.

Pampas grass hails from the South American grasslands of Brazil, Argentina, and Chile. Although it's not indigenous to our southeast, pampas grass thrives like a native. That's because its home climate has hot, often rainless summers, with enough humidity to make you think you're in Charleston on an August afternoon. The winters in its native habitat are relatively mild, even by our southern standards.

Pampas Grass
Cortaderia selloana

It's too bad that pampas grass remains one of the most misunderstood plants in a gardener's plant palette. That's because few people really understand what pampas grass is going to do when they plant it. Most folks pick a spot for pampas grass and think that it will add a beautiful accent to their landscape. And it does—for the first year or two. Then they find themselves engulfed by this monstrous grass taking more room than they wanted it to, or had allowed for. Of course, everyone has seen "The Twins" at the end of the driveway.

The other misuse of pampas grass is a phenomenon we call "a pampas island unto itself." Most everyone has seen that lonely, solitary clump of pampas grass standing tall and proud in a green sea of lawn. Of course, it has no purpose, such as tying a visual dimension to the landscape, or accenting a line that draws the eye to another vista.

Do try to remember that a plant as big as pampas grass should be used where it has room to grow. It is best used as a transitional plant that will take us from one part of the landscape to the next, or as a screen for hiding unsightly views. The last pampas grass principle is to use odd numbers. As much as it galls Brian's symmetrical disposition, even he admits that using plants in odd numbers creates a more pleasing visual effect than even numbers. So, unless you are creating a very formal garden, like an English one, plant in odd numbers.

Pampas grass does best in full sun, but it will grow in shade if you're willing to accept noticeably reduced flowering. A common development over time is that a stand of pampas grass shades itself in the center and ends up with a donut hole. This is usually not an aesthetic problem because tall grass hides the dead middle. However, regular cutting back of the grass in the spring, dividing the clump when it gets too large, as well as grabbing and pulling out the dead stalks will keep the center from rotting. Be forewarned, though. The grass blades are razor-sharp and will cut you. We strongly recommend wearing long pants, a long-sleeved shirt, and gloves when working with this plant. Also, stuff your pants legs into your socks, and try to seal every opening in your clothing, because a blade of pampas grass can find a way inside your clothes and drive you crazy.

There are many types of pampas grass to choose from. You can find it in variegated, silver striped, yellow striped, even purplish- and pink-blooming varieties. Just remember that size can become a problem in many garden situations. However, a little-known and woefully underused variety, 'Pumila', is compact (about 4–6 feet tall) and much better suited for most gardens than the standard species.

Height: 7–10 feet • Spread: 6–8 feet • Sun: best in full sun, but grows in shade • Moisture: takes it all • Hardiness Zone: varies with variety, ranges from 6–12 • Heat Zone: 5–12 (estimated) • Propagation: division of clumps

Lemon Grass

Cymbopogon citratus

How often does one find a great ornamental that can also be eaten? With its long and flowing wide blades, Lemon Grass offers us texture and fragrance in the garden as well as flavor in the kitchen. This cold-sensitive grass is truly one of the great sleepers in herbs and ornamental grasses.

Lemon Grass is considered an annual for most *Some Like It Hot* gardeners. Only those of us who live in USDA Zones 8b and higher can get it to overwinter outside. The rest of us must place a few plants in the greenhouse.

The blades emanate from the center of the clump. The new ones emerge straight up, while the older leaves droop back over the clump, often touching the ground. These plants are especially effective in a container. We suggest terra cotta because the color contrast between the leaf blades and the pot is quite attractive.

When Lemon Grass is crushed, it gives off a fragrant but not overpowering lemony smell. The scent comes from the release of aromatic oils stored in the leaf blades. (It should come as no surprise that Lemon Grass is first cousin to *C. nardus*, the source of citronella oil.)

As far as its tolerance of hot humid conditions, this plant was born in them! The hot humid conditions of its native habitat are some of the most brutal on earth. During the summer, Charlestonians are regularly subjected to 95° F and 95% humidity. Our highs and lows often match New Delhi, India's during July and August. Lemon Grass, which is native to southern India and Sri Lanka (formerly Ceylon), can easily take Mumbai's (formerly Bombay) summer temperatures of 105° F with 100% humidity. Now that's hot and humid! So when your summer heat and humidity gets to whatever your definition of unbearable is, Lemon Grass just smiles happily.

Lemon Grass is one of those plants that likes regular moisture and prefers full sun. However, it is rather indifferent to soil types. It seems to handle any soil from sand to clay as long as it has enough sun and some water. We recommend growing Lemon Grass in full sun where the most brutal heat of the day can warm its hot-blooded sap, and near enough to the sprinkler so it can lap up water at its leisure.

Height: 2–3 feet • Spread: 1–2 feet • Sun: full sun • Moisture: prefers regular watering • Hardiness Zone: 9–12 • Heat Zone: 7–12 (estimated) • Propagation: division before winter

Japanese Blood Grass
Imperata cylindrica 'Rubra'
Japanese Blood Grass is a nice plant to add to one's ornamental grass palette. Its wide blades and bright red leaves can make a significant impact in the landscape. Underground rhizomes send up green blades with red tips in spring and as warm weather settles in, the color deepens and increases to all but the lowest 3 or 4 inches of the leaf blade. (Occasionally, some of the clumps will revert to the green form. When this occurs, just remove them to maintain a fully-colored species.) We have never seen Japanese Blood Grass in bloom, but hor-

ticulture literature describes a silky white flower head up to 2 feet long. Its occurrence is rare.

This is a great plant for the water-conscious gardener. Once established, Japanese Blood Grass is very drought-tolerant and can take a good bit of abuse, although it performs best in fertile soils with good moisture and full sun. It can easily be propagated from clump division in the spring.

We think Japanese Blood Grass looks best planted in mass. Unless you are growing a single clump in a container, it won't create that all-important visual impact that most folks want from ornamental grasses. Even small gardens can achieve visual pizzazz by planting five to seven clumps close together. Of course, fifteen to thirty plants will create a more dramatic mass. But for gardens of any size, remember the odd-number rule.

Japanese Blood Grass is native to lowland areas of Japan, China, Korea, and Manchuria. When you look at these areas on a map, you'll see they share many geographic features with the eastern U.S. seaboard. This is one of the reasons it performs so well for many deep south gardeners.

Height: 20 inches • Spread: 6–8 inches • Sun: full sun • Moisture: prefers moist soil, but drought-tolerant once established • Hardiness Zone: 6–10 • Heat Zone: 5–11 (estimated) • Propagation: rhizomes

Liriope, Monkey Grass, Lilyturf

Liriope spp.

Good old ubiquitous liriope. It's been so extensively used as a garden border that it's become a mandatory accessory in every southern landscape. Well, why not? Liriope tolerates very dry soils and has few pest problems. And it grows where lawn grasses won't, and it doesn't croak in winter. (But why do we like having dark green borders accentuate our dead plants in January?) Unfortunately, liriope has been so over-used that most of us have forgotten its original merits.

Liriope
Liriope spp.

Liriope
Liriope spp.

Liriopes are too often used as a one-plant-deep border around beds or walkways. What a shame! We recommend cultivating this ornamental grass all by itself in large, sweeping elliptical beds. After all, it can be treated like a groundcover and it looks marvelous when it's planted in staggered masses. If you feel compelled to use it as a border, then why not plant it in bold sweeping curves instead of straight lines?

Liriope also looks great planted on an incline or under large shade trees where competition for water and nutrients prevents other plants from thriving. It sends up a purple or lavender flower spike in early summer, and blue/black berries appear in early fall.

While it is not required, mowing in the late winter to early spring is a good maintenance practice. If the plants are accessible, set your lawn mower height to about three inches and catch the clippings in the bagger. Although many recommend dividing liriope in the spring, P.J. completes this chore whenever she gets around to it. She has even rearranged masses of liriope during the dog days of August and not one blade wilted. Another maintenance advantage to the liriopes is they are able to tolerate direct applications of many grassy herbicides. When grassy weeds invade a liriope planting, spraying the area with something like Vantage® will kill them but not harm the liriope.

When you look at our *Some Like It Hot* plant list, you'll find that we've included several species of liriope. While they all share the same cultural aspects, they vary in size and looks. We think these differences need explanation because many gardeners associate height and color with overall plant health. *L. muscari*, the most widely used liriope, stands about 1–1^1/$_2$ feet tall and has a less than ^{1}/$_2$-inch-wide leaf blade. The cultivar 'Big Blue' is a darker color than *L. muscari*. So don't assume your plants need more fertilizer just because they aren't a deep green like your neighbors'. You may be comparing the standard, lighter green muscari with its lusher cousin.

L. spicata stands about 1–1^1/$_2$ feet tall but has a much narrower leaf blade, about ^{1}/$_4$ inch. *L. grandiflora* is the largest of the liriopes. It reaches 2 feet in height and has the widest leaf blades at ^{1}/$_2$ inch or more.

Height: 1^1/$_2$–2 feet • Spread: 8–12 inches (L. spicata spreads profusely with underground rhizomes) • Sun: full sun or shade • Moisture: tolerates dry soil • Hardiness Zone: 6–10 • Heat Zone: 6–12 (estimated) • Propagation: division of clumps in the spring

Miscanthus, Maidenhair Grass

Miscanthus spp.

The botanical name for this grass, *Miscanthus*, comes from two Greek words: *mischos* means stalk, and *anthos* means flower. Together the words refer to the long stalks with a flower head at the end.

Miscanthus is the total package when it comes to a *Some Like It Hot* plant. Its native habitat is the marshy coastal regions, slopes, and mountainsides of eastern Asia, with a few species native to west Africa. This plant truly loves heat and humidity. In fact, it requires hot weather to set the gorgeous flowers we all have come to associate with this grass. It enjoys some of the most brutal hot and humid weather we can subject it to. Granted, it does well in the drier Mediterranean-like climate of California, but it thrives in the humid southeast. And this brings us to the rub: It thrives a little too well in hot humid climates.

Miscanthus has the potential to be invasive. From discussions with horti-culturists from the northeast, Brian has learned that Miscanthus is being con-sidered for placement on the "Noxious Weed" list in some northeastern states. Notwithstanding its invasive potential, Miscanthus *is* a good ornamental grass. The flowers of Miscanthus create textured beauty in the landscape. The diver-sity of this plant is amazing, with over a hundred cultivars and species. More hybrids are sure to come. You can find wide- and narrow-leaf types (referred to as coarse and fine-textured), variegated, plus variations of leaf color. If you really want to know everything about the Miscanthus species and its cultivars,

Morning Light Miscanthus
Miscanthus sinensis
'Morning Light'

Cosmopolitan Miscanthus
Miscanthus sinensis
'Cosmopolitan'

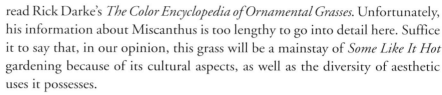

read Rick Darke's *The Color Encyclopedia of Ornamental Grasses*. Unfortunately, his information about Miscanthus is too lengthy to go into detail here. Suffice it to say that, in our opinion, this grass will be a mainstay of *Some Like It Hot* gardening because of its cultural aspects, as well as the diversity of aesthetic uses it possesses.

Miscanthus
Miscanthus sinensis

You can use Miscanthus as a feature plant in containers. Its tall flower stalks and flowing blades make it an excellent focal plant in container arrangements. It thrives in hostile conditions, so if you forget to water the pot, it will still be there when you finally remember to check the container. Miscanthus also works great as an accent plant along water. Again, its hardiness in hot dry weather means it can withstand long periods of no rainfall, yet keep a nice appearance. This is an important consideration when choosing plants for water settings. When plants are reflected in the water, you see the good or the bad twice. Needless to say, you want plants that will continue to look attractive during bad times.

In spite of its marvelous uses in containers and along waterways, it is the mass plantings of Miscanthus that make it truly outstanding. These plantings make excellent landscape screens. However, always remember that Miscanthus has the potential to become invasive. Every region has a unique threshold, so check with a local horticulturist before using Miscanthus in your garden.

Height: varies with variety/species 3–8 feet • Spread: varies with variety/species 1–6 feet • Sun: full sun • Moisture: likes moist soil but will tolerate dry conditions • Hardiness Zone: varies 4–12 • Heat Zone: 5–12 (estimated) • Propagation: depends on species/variety

Sweetgrass, Pink Muhly
Muhlenbergia capillaris
Sweetgrass, Purple Muhly
Muhlenbergia filipes

Pink Muhly Sweetgrass
Muhlenbergia capillaris

There are several plants associated with "southernness." Magnolias and Spanish-moss-draped live oaks usually top the list. However, there is a genus of ornamental grass that unequivocally exemplifies the history and lore of coastal South Carolina. We encourage you to try it in your landscape. It's called sweetgrass, and it grows wild in coastal dunes from North Carolina to Florida and Texas, then into Mexico down to the Yucatan Peninsula. Charleston's basket makers use the slender leaves to weave exquisite containers. It's an African craft that's been handed down from one generation to the next for over three hundred years.

Sweetgrass in parts of the South Carolina lowcountry is disappearing from the wild. Land development on Charleston's barrier islands has depleted sweetgrass availability, and conservationists are beginning to take notice.

Muhlenbergia includes over 125 species. Although we're interested in only two of them, as a plantsman, Brian finds all of *Muhlenbergia* fascinating because it's native to the arid prairies of the west as well as the humid coastal plains of the southeast. While some plant taxonomists split out the arid and coastal types as separate species, the differences are practically on a microscopic level. You and we cannot tell *M. filipes* and *M. capillaris* apart no matter how hard we look at them.

If you are not familiar with this plant, you are in for a real treat! Sweetgrass has very fine-textured, narrow-leaf blades that are a dark green color during the growing season. They can add a wonderful fine-textured accent to the garden throughout the summer. It is during the fall, however, that this plant glows with beauty and appeal. Starting in the early fall, sweetgrass will produce long flower stalks that rise above the grass blades. Then, toward the middle of fall, *M. capillaris*'s flower spikes burst open with very soft fine pink flowers. The flowers are so fine that they look as if they are glowing. (Think of the soft appearance that you see when someone is wearing a fur coat and stands in front of a light so the coat edges are backlighted.) Purple Muhly produces the same effect—floating clouds of color that appear to hover above the foliage. The beauty is enthralling no matter how many times one has seen it.

Muhlys are an open-area plant. Here in Charleston, they grow wild in ditch banks and areas where moisture is plentiful with lots of sun. This is the kind of environment you should choose for sweetgrass in your landscape. Pick an area that has full sun with adequate moisture—otherwise you will need to irrigate often. Because the flowers are so fine-textured, it is important to have several clumps massed together to create one large, thick planting. Sweetgrass is a plant with fairly decent cold tolerance. It can safely grow as far north as USDA Zone 6, and with some protection, even further north. Muhlys are wonderfully beautiful plants and we wish that everyone could have the opportunity to enjoy their beauty.

Height: 2 feet • Spread: 1–2 feet • Sun: full sun • Moisture: supply ample moisture • Hardiness Zone: 6–10 • Heat Zone: 7–12 (estimated) • Propagation: seeds or division in spring

Mondo Grass
Ophiopogon japonicus

Mondo Grass is a plant with a lot of potential, yet is underutilized by gardeners. It tolerates many of the same conditions as liriope, but has a very fine-textured leaf and is much shorter. Mondo Grass deserves a place in many landscapes but its full potential is still waiting to be discovered by gardeners and professional horticulturists.

Mondo Grass
Ophiopogon japonicus

Mondo Grass is very dark green and the color doesn't weaken when it's planted in the shade. Many of us have spots in our gardens that are just too shaded for much to grow. Mondo Grass is the answer for these troublesome areas. And if you have enough room, we suggest the following mix for a dramatic shade garden: plant Mondo in the foreground area, then combine Oakleaf Hydrangeas with their purple foliage, and variegated gardenias with their yellow foliage in the background. This combination will give you stunning color in the shade when the hydrangeas and the gardenias are in bloom.

Mondo Grass is a clumping grass that stands about 6 inches tall. Its narrow dark green leaves do best in shade, but can tolerate sun in many areas of the U.S., with AHS Heat Zones 10 and up being the exceptions. *O. japonicas* 'Nana', a dwarf cultivar, literally hugs the ground at only 2–3 inches in height.

Height: 4–6 feet • Spread: 3–4 feet • Sun: shade • Moisture: tolerates dry conditions • Hardiness Zone: 7–10 • Heat Zone: 5–10 (estimated) • Propagation: division

Switch-Grass, Panic Grass
Panicum virgatum

Panic grasses are made up of about six hundred species, and Switch-Grass is the category of importance to us. When someone refers to panic grass in the garden, they really mean Switch-Grass.

Switch-Grass is a homeboy. Native to North America, it's found everywhere except California, the northwest, and Mexico. It tolerates wet or dry conditions and all kinds of soils. Switch-Grass is easy to grow as long as it's allowed 4–5 hours of sunlight a day. Put it anywhere you want, but do pay attention to the light requirement. A cold-hardy plant that grows well in the north (USDA Zone 4), Switch-Grass growing in warmer climes sometimes gets heat-related diseases. Gardeners in the AHS Heat Zone 9 or higher should keep a watch out for rust.

Switch-Grass
Panicum virgatum

Growing Switch-Grass can make anyone look like a pro. You'll be hard pressed to find a plant that is easier to grow. This characteristic makes it a great grass for the self-proclaimed "brown thumb" or the novice who needs a little confidence-booster. It also makes an excellent gift for someone whose climate is unfamiliar to you.

Most Switch-Grasses are upright with dark green leaves. The flowers are airy panicles with different colors based on the variety. We suggest trying 'Prairie Skies' or 'Cloud Nine'.

Height: 6–8 feet • Spread: 3–4 feet • Sun: full sun • Moisture: prefers regular moisture • Hardiness Zone: 4–10 • Heat Zone: 4–12 (estimated) • Propagation: seeds or division

Fountain Grass
Pennisetum alopecuroides

The fountain grasses are our favorite ornamental grasses. The botanical name *Pennisetum* comes from two Latin words, *penna* meaning feather, and *seta* meaning bristle. Fountain grasses do just what the name implies, they produce fountains of flowers emanating from clumps of grass. The flowers will start as erect flower heads and then cascade to the ground as they age. All the while, new flowers emerge erect and tall. The result is a fountain appearance.

Native to the lowlands of Japan and eastern Asia, fountain grasses are right at home along the eastern seaboard of the U.S. They really love hot, humid weather and they actually wait for the heat of June to begin flowering. Tolerant of a wide degree of soil types, they will do well if planted in full sun and receive regular watering.

These plants have good cold tolerance, grow well into USDA Zone 6, and will perform admirably in AHS Heat Zones 4–11. They make great screens on berms, and look nice at the bottom of the hill along the water's edge—or anywhere in between. However, this species of fountain grass is not suited for specimen planting. Instead, they are most effective when massed together or used in a mixed planting scheme of three to five.

You can find fountain grass in a variety of colors and forms. Just take the time to learn about the different varieties and then choose the one best suited for your situation.

Height: 3–5 feet, depending on variety • Spread: 2–4 feet • Sun: full sun or light shade • Moisture: regular moisture is best, but can tolerate drought • Hardiness Zone: 6–10 • Heat Zone: 5–11 (estimated) • Propagation: division, can use seeds with straight species

Purple Fountain Grass

P. setaceum 'Rubrum' or *P. alopecuroides* 'Rubrum'

This is our favorite fountain grass. Its purple leaves, with flowers flowing from the center of the clump, simply send us into rapture. Unfortunately, this plant is very cold-sensitive. Native to tropical Africa, southwestern Asia, and Arabia, it does not tolerate cold weather. Temperatures around 35° F are about all it can take. This means that folks in USDA Zone 9 may treat it as a perennial

Purple Fountain Grass
Pennisetum setaceum
'Rubrum'

while those in Zone 8 may be able to squeak by with some protection. The rest of us have to love it as an annual plant.

Purple Fountain Grass blooms in the early summer and lasts until frost. Since it rarely sets seed, propagate Purple Fountain Grass by digging up and dividing clumps in the early winter. Store them in a greenhouse or garage until spring.

Purple Fountain Grass reaches 5 feet tall with 1-foot flowers. 'East Canyon' is a compact form of 'Rubrum' that reaches only 30 inches tall. It too is an all-around performer and can be used just like any other fountain grass—along berms or waterways, and in masses or small groups of three to five.

Purple Fountain Grass also makes a good specimen plant. One of its best uses is as a centerpiece in a container planting. Whether it's a medium-sized concrete urn or one of those huge planters that are almost as big as some city gardens, Purple Fountain Grass's color and texture will definitely be the star of the pot.

Some doubt exists as to which species Purple Fountain Grass actually belongs, so we have listed it in both names in case you look in books that may use only one of the names. It seems the *P. alopecuroides* 'Rubrum' is the most commonly used name among horticulturists.

Height: 5 feet (30 inches for 'East Canyon')
• Spread: 2–3 feet • Sun: full sun • Moisture: needs regular moisture • Hardiness Zone: 9–12 • Heat Zone: 7–12 (estimated) • Propagation: division before winter

Purple Fountain Grass
Pennisetum setaceum
'Rubrum'

Annual Vines

While we consider most herbaceous annuals to be a nuisance, we're quite fond of annual vines. It seems to us that many annuals are just too seasonally specific. In other words, their growing and blooming periods are short. Plant primroses in the spring and they're gone before the end of May.

Yellow Bleeding Heart
Dicentra scandens

Sweet William (*Dianthus barbatus*) may last a little longer, but not much. Herbaceous annuals can also be high-maintenance plants. We love pansies as much as everyone else does, but spending most of the winter picking off spent blossoms so they'll keep blooming through April can wear thin. We even know folks who replant zinnias several times during the summer. That's too much work for us, but, thankfully, annual vines are different. They're robust, full-season plants. Start them in the spring after the danger of frost has passed, then walk away from them. They will bloom from summer through fall and all the way to first frost. Many of them can reach heights of 10 feet or more in just a couple of months. When the first freeze finally arrives, annual vines die back completely, leaving only seeds which, in some cases, will assure new plants in the spring.

Vines do not have a true growth habit. This is an advantage for gardeners because we get to choose what shape the vine will eventually take. Unlike shrubs, which have erect, weeping, or broad growth habits if allowed to grow at their own pace, vines will take on whatever form is available. If allowed to grow on a fence, they will eventually acquire a broad habit. Put that same vine near a pole and it will grow upward and erect. And when they reach the top of a wall and have nothing to grab onto, they will cascade down the other side and take on a weeping effect.

Now, before you start thinking that you can do just any old thing to any old vine, allow us to explain a few more things about them. They're not quite as pliable as we just made them out to be. At the risk of anthropomorphizing, these guys have minds of their own, and you'll have to understand their rules if you want to win at the vine game. Although the following could be titled "Basic Vine Botany 101," don't let the science stuff scare you off. This is fascinating!

Vines are terrifically phototropic. In other words, they will only grow toward light. If you are determined to get a vine to grow in an easterly direction, but that part of your garden receives more abundant afternoon sun from the west, all the staking and tying and fertilizing won't change your plant's direction of growth. It will grow toward the west since the light is stronger from that direction. This is because plants have hormones called auxins. When the leaves and stems are exposed to light, the auxins travel from the light-receiving side to the darker side. The lopsided concentration of auxins causes the plant to bend toward the light. (Some vines are so light-sensitive that they follow the sun's movement. This is called heliotropism.)

There are basically two kinds of vines: clinging and non-clinging. Clinging vines grab with holdfasts or suction cups. Non-clingers (and all of our *Some Like It Hot* annual vines are in this category), climb by using a twisting action in the stems and/or tendrils. Twining vines wrap their stems around whatever is available for support. Botanically speaking, the spiraling action is called circumnutation and the spiraling direction is genetically predetermined. Some vines twine clockwise, others counterclockwise. Have you ever wound a vine around a pole only to find it back on the ground a few hours later? You probably wound it in the wrong direction. If you don't believe us, then try this. Grow a morning glory in a hanging basket and place a dowel in the center for it to twine on. Now hang the pot upside down and watch what happens. The vine will uncurl and rearrange itself to adapt to its new position!

Most vines twine in a counterclockwise direction. However, if you're not sure whether you have a Japanese or Chinese wisteria, look at its twining direction. *W. floribunda* or Japanese wisteria twines counterclockwise while *W. sinensis* wraps from left to right. If vines had hands, then we know of only one with ambidexterity. The tropical plant *Loasa* will twine in either direction.

Some non-clinging vines, such as Coral Vine and Passionflower, lack the stem strength to climb on their own. So how does a vine get to the sunlight if it keeps flopping over? They modify their stems or leaves into tendrils. These

Yellow Bleeding Heart
Dicentra scandens

thready, spring-like appendages will grab onto anything they meet. In fact, time-lapse photography demonstrates that the tendril tips make sweeping motions as they search for something to touch. Once an object is found, it takes only a few seconds to coil around it. Keep this information in mind when training vines with tendrils. If the vine starts to grow into a treasured plant (P.J.'s Coral Vine simply loves her 'Yellow Galaxy' chrysanthemums), you might have a frustrating time untangling the mess.

Many gardeners, and we are guilty of this too, use the same plants repeatedly, never daring to try new ones for lack of knowledge or courage. We can all benefit from expanding our plant palette when using vines. When was the last time you experimented with new ways to grow a vine? Why not try a cascading fountain or weeping effect? Instead of having just a pole or string extending into the air, add a flat plate or ring of wire at the top and train the vine up the pole and over the cap piece. Or instead of planting a vine on the wall facing your house, plant it on the opposite side and let it run over the top and cascade down to make a flowering waterfall. This planting technique also works on an arbor.

Since all of our *Some Like It Hot* annual vines may be propagated from seed, we would be remiss if we didn't include a discussion about germination. One of the things that drives us nuts is the scant information some seed companies put on the backs of their seed packets. Some seeds, such as *Dicentra scandens* and *Aristolochia* spp., need light to germinate. However, this vital information is often excluded from the sowing instructions.

We have included a Seed Planting Guide at the end of this chapter. Although we mention propagation information after each plant discussion, our chart offers a more detailed analysis of every plant's germination characteristics. If you are planning to sow a lot of different kinds of seed in a heated bed, this will help you organize the planting arrangement.

So, where does one find reliable seed? There are numerous, reputable seed companies to choose from. (See our list at the back of this book.) Many have websites and some have toll-free numbers for customers with gardening questions. However, don't overlook local gardening centers. If they don't carry what you are looking for, they may be more willing to help you find it than the mega-hardware/garden stores.

We also suggest collecting seeds from a friend or neighbor, then extending the kindness to others after you have established your own plants. Some annual vines, such as *Antigonon leptopus*, produce abundant amounts of seeds. It seems foolish to us to order Coral Vine from a seed catalog when they are so plentiful in Charleston gardens.

Harvesting seed is not a mysterious art that only a chosen few know how to do. Just remember that for a seed to be viable, and therefore germinate, it must be fully developed. (If you've ever carefully collected green bell pepper seeds and then wondered why you never got a new crop of peppers, it's because the seeds weren't fully developed. Allow the green bell to turn red. The seeds will be viable after the fruit turns red.) It's pretty easy to know when annual vine seeds are ripe. You will find seedpods where flowers once bloomed. Wait until the pods turn brownish or tan and practically fall off the vine when you touch them. Gently crumble a pod in your hand and the seeds should dislodge.

Some Like It Hot Annual Vines

Antigonon leptopus	Coral Vine
Aristolochia elegans	Calico Flower
A. durior	Dutchman's Pipe
Clerodendrum splendens	Bleeding Heart Vine
Clitoria ternatea 'Blue Sails'	Blue Sails Vine
Cobaea scandens	Cup-and-Saucer Vine
Dicentra scandens	Yellow Bleeding Heart Vine
Dolichos lablab	Hyacinth Bean, Lablab
Syn. *Lablab purpureus*	
Ipomoea alba	Moonvine
I. tricolor	Morning Glory
I. × multifida	Cardinal Vine
Mandevilla spp.	Mandevilla
Mascagnia macroptera	Yellow Orchid Vine, Butterfly Vine
Passiflora spp.	Passionflower
Phaseolus coccineus	Scarlet Runner Bean, Jefferson Plant
Pseudogynoxys chenopodioides	Mexican Flame Vine
Syn. *Senecio confusus*	
Thunbergia alata	Black-Eyed Susan Vine
T. grandiflora	Blue Sky Vine, Blue Indian Vine
T. gregorii	Orange Clock Vine
Vigna caracalla	Snail Vine, Caracalla Bean
Syn. *Phaseolus caracalla*	

Cardinal Vine
Ipomoea × multifida

Once you've collected the seed and planted it, you assume that you'll get exactly what you were growing the season before, right? Well, maybe not. One of our *Some Like It Hot* annual vines, *Ipomoea × multifida*, is a hybrid, which means that it has two different parents. The Cardinal Vine is a cross between the Red Morning Glory and the Cypress Vine. When these two come together, they produce progeny with what is called "hybrid vigor." This means that each parent's good qualities suppress the not-so-good ones. This result, designated an F1 hybrid because it is the first generation, gives us a stunning annual vine. However, the seeds produced by the F1 hybrid are second generation (F2) ones. These seeds are not good. If you planted them, you'd end up with a genetically mixed hodgepodge of very undesirable vines because, this time, the unattractive traits show up. So, whenever you hear someone say that a certain plant won't breed true, they're talking about an F1 hybrid. By the way, the International Code of Botanical Nomenclature designated the multiplication symbol × for hybrid plants. Not meant to be read or spoken, its position within a botanical name is like a genetic identification code for horticulturists. However, all we gardeners need to know is that the × means the plant is a hybrid.

Some of these plants are probably very familiar to you, while others will be new finds. As always, the best part about any plant is the discovery, whether it is a new one or a rediscovery. One note on the cultural information we include with each plant: Vines don't really have a defined height and spread. They grow as high and as wide as the structure you put them on. Therefore, we have not included height and spread information although we sometimes mention potential length in our discussions.

Coral Vine

Antigonon leptopus

We can never get enough of this plant. Coral Vine rewards us with non-stop blooming clumps of pink-ish flowers from mid- to late summer, then continues for what seems like forever. However, there is more to this plant's ornamental value than interesting flowers. The rough-textured, lime green, heart-shaped leaves also contribute to its overall beauty. While Brian prefers the look of southern wildness when masses of Coral Vine are allowed to assault a large wall, P.J. is content to grow more modest amounts along a wrought-iron fence.

Coral Vine
Antigonon leptopus

A native of Mexico, Coral Vine is tolerant of heat and humidity and that is why it's grown extensively in the southeast and along the Gulf Coast. But what really makes this plant special is its toughness. It's one of those urban jungle survivors that takes the rigors of a city environment quite well. It tolerates drought, poor soil, almost no soil, and air pollution. If you live in the city, chances are that you have a postage-stamp-sized yard. As long as it receives full sun, Coral Vine can turn a troublesome 1-foot by 3-foot bare spot into an attractive area. It will also survive in the space between your property and the public sidewalk, that no-man's-land you more than likely own, but which the city maintains the divine right to rip asunder. The ground is quite hard there and the exhaust fumes are relentless. An additional benefit of Coral Vine is its propensity to attract butterflies. It also has an intoxicating effect on bees. If there is a drawback to this plant, it is the sun requirement. Don't waste your time putting it in a semi-shaded spot. You'll be lucky to get even one spindly shoot. And if you do, don't count on that scraggly thing to head for the sun and fill out. It won't. *All* of Coral Vine needs full sun to grow and produce flowers.

While it is a perennial in USDA Zones 9–10, it often sneaks by in protected areas of Zone 8. In places where you can establish it as a perennial it will grow as much as 30–40 feet. For the rest of us who must treat it as an annual, it will cover a 10–15 foot wall each season even if it starts over from the ground.

Climbing method: tendrils • Sun: full sun • Moisture: tolerates drought very well, although flowering will be reduced • Hardiness Zone: 9–10 • Heat Zone: 5–12 • Propagation: seeds or rooted cuttings

Calico Flower
Aristolochia elegans
Dutchman's Pipe
A. durior

Calico Flower and Dutchman's Pipe are bittersweet. In other words, we have some good news and some not-so-good news about them. *Aristolochias* have large, S-shaped flowers that look like Sherlock Holmes's pipe. Of course, this attribute is an ornamental plus, and the unusual flower color—speckled purple to brown on vague light green—results in a showy mottled appearance. It's not the kind of flower you'd expect to find in many gardens. The foliage is equally splendid with quite large, dark green, heart-shaped leaves. They provide a striking background for the calabash-pipe-like flowers. The profusion of blooms in summer makes this plant almost irresistible. And one of the most appealing characteristics about *Aristolochia* is that it's a fast-growing, shade-loving plant.

Did you notice that we said *almost* irresistible? The flowers of most *Aristolochias* emit a powerful redolence that smells like rotting meat. Female flies, attracted to this malodorous smell, zoom in to lay eggs. The tubular flowers are lined with fine, reverse-angled hairs, and when the fly is ready to leave, she has to struggle to get out. As she wiggles around to escape, she inadvertently pollinates the flower. We have been told that the tropical *Aristolochia*s smell worse than others do. However, Calico Flower and Dutchman's Pipe both give off this unpleasant odor and we're not interested in discerning their differences.

Obviously, the best use of this vine is in a shady spot where you can see it from a distance but rarely need to pass near it. The plant grows very rapidly, reaching 10–12 feet in one season. Its large foliage makes it one that needs a strong support. It will tightly twine around its support, which makes it an excellent screening vine for a chainlink fence. The unpleasant odor of this beautiful vine is a challenge to overcome. Nonetheless, we believe its ornamental value, especially the shade tolerance, makes it worth trying, although establishing a level of odor tolerance may present a problem.

Climbing method: twining stems • Sun: partial shade to filtered shade • Moisture: needs regular watering • Hardiness Zone: 9–10, protected areas of 8 • Heat Zone: 3–12 • Propagation: seeds and cuttings or air-layered stems

Bleeding Heart Vine
Clerodendrum splendens
Almost all of the *Clerodendrums* are native to tropical Africa. While this makes them great plants for hot and humid weather, they absolutely refuse to tolerate anything below freezing.

Bleeding Heart Vine is a common name used for two different *Clerodendrum* species. This is why common names drive horticulturists crazy. *C. thomsoniae* is a greenhouse, conservatory, indoor vine whose flowers have white sepals and crimson petals. *C. splendens*, whose common name is also Bleeding Heart Vine, is the species we are concerned with. We know of no other common name to distinguish the two, and it would be nice if someone with common naming authority gave us separate names to distinguish these plants. *C. splendens* has scarlet flowers but no white sepals. It is a relatively fast grower and can cover a pole or short fence easily during the growing season.

Climbing method: twining stems • Sun: full sun • Moisture: regular moisture • Hardiness Zone: 10–11 • Heat Zone: 4–12 • Propagation: seeds or rooted cuting

Blue Sails Vine
Clitoria ternatea 'Blue Sails'

Clitoria ternatea 'Blue Sails' is rarely used in U.S. gardens. It's a beautiful vine with semi-double dark blue flowers. This vine is a variety. The straight species has single dark blue flowers. They are both members of a genus that has over seventy species, most of them originating from tropical Asia. Consequently, they like our summers but don't care very much for the winters. While they will come back from the roots in Zones 9–11, and maybe in Zone 8 with protection, they really are an annual plant. Fortunately, they will return from seed quite easily. This vine will grow about 10 feet during the season but it depends on where you are. If you are a plant-trivia-oriented gardener, here is an interesting side note about the species name *ternatea*. Normally, when the Latin word *ternate* is used, it refers to three leaves. This plant, however, has compound leaves made up of 5–7 leaflets. The name *ternatea* comes from the plant's origin, the island of Ternate in Indonesia, which sits right on the equator. Now you know why it hates our winters.

Climbing method: twining stems • Sun: full sun • Moisture: regular moisture • Hardiness Zone: 9–11 • Heat Zone: 5–12 (estimated) • Propagation: seeds in the spring

Cup-and-Saucer Vine
Cobaea scandens

The flowers on a Cup-and-Saucer Vine really do look like cups and saucers. Well, at least they did to the person who gave it the name. It's a visually fascinating flower because the large calyx is so showy. Notwithstanding the novelty factor, the flower is very beautiful and quite large. It can reach as much as 3–5 inches across which means the Cup-and-Saucer Vine makes a big impact wherever it is used. Although we have no first-hand experience with this vine, we are confident that its large flowers will prohibit its use in small or closed areas. Brian also believes that the plant would look too aggressive in a narrow path or alley. Of course, if that's the kind of look you're after, then Cup-and-Saucer Vine is the right choice. However, we suggest its best aesthetic appeal will be in a large open space. Place it in an area where the large flowers will attract attention from a distance, or allow it to serve as a focal point when viewed from your porch.

We must warn you of *C. scandens*'s growth rate. Cup-and-Saucer vine can grow as much as 15–30 feet in one season. This native of the Mexican mountains likes full sun. However, it will tolerate some shade, although flowering will probably be reduced. As for its culture, provide plenty of water, no nitrogen, and something strong for it to climb on.

Climbing method: twining stems • Sun: full sun • Moisture: regular moisture • Hardiness Zone: 9–11 • Heat Zone: 1–10 (estimated) • Propagation: seeds in the spring (soak overnight)

Yellow Bleeding Heart Vine

Dicentra scandens

Yellow Bleeding Heart Vine is a very different plant from the traditional Bleeding Heart vines. The Bleeding Heart most gardeners are familiar with is *Clerodendrum splendens*. Yellow Bleeding Heart is in a different genus and has very different characteristics. It has smaller leaves with yellow flowers and has an affinity to shade. That doesn't mean the shade under the eave on the north side of the house, because that kind of deep shade will not satisfy this plant. Yellow Bleeding Heart Vine prefers filtered sunlight most of the day. However, if it's planted under a tree, or in an area that gets at most an hour or two of full sun and then receives only filtered sunlight during the rest of the day, it probably won't sulk. If you have tried to grow plants in a similar deeply-shaded area but have been disappointed with the lack of flowers, or failed to get a single one, then you will be amazed at the profusion of flowers you'll receive from the Yellow Bleeding Heart Vine. Although the Yellow Bleeding Heart will flower in any most-day shade, it does better if you can give it morning sun and

Yellow Bleeding
Heart Vine
Dicentra scandens

only afternoon shade. The one thing you don't want to do is place it in full sun. Although we expect someone to pull us up short by claiming they do exactly that and have no problem, it is the exception and not the norm.

We almost excluded Yellow Bleeding Heart from this annual vine chapter. It's not really an annual vine, but more of a perennial. It dies back to the ground at first frost then comes back from the roots the following spring. It is root-hardy in Asheville, NC. In the lower ends of Zone 9, it can actually make it through the winter without dieback if the weather is mild enough.

Climbing method: twining stems • Sun: morning sun / filtered shade • Moisture: regular moisture • Hardiness Zone: 7–11 • Heat Zone: 3–12 (estimated) • Propagation: seeds or rooted cuttings

Hyacinth Bean

Dolichos lablab Syn. *Lablab purpureus*

Hyacinth Bean is a vine that is becoming as commonplace and almost as well known as the morning glory. It's a great plant for the beginner who is trying to gain some confidence with annual plants. The beans germinate easily when they are planted in pots or directly into the ground. These vines grow rapidly and are resistant to pests. In midsummer, purple to lavender flowers emerge, followed by purple bean pods. The pods can be as interesting as the flowers and, for the culinarily-inclined, Hyacinth Beans hold more than ornamental value. The pods are edible when young and fresh or after they have been allowed to dry. They are commonly used as a food source in the tropics.

Hyacinth Bean is a vine that needs strong support. The typical bamboo pole that most vines are given to grow on will not support the weight of a mature Hyacinth Bean plant. Metal structures are usually best. Of course, you can always plant it near a tree or shrub and just let it grow up and into the woody plant. Once it reaches the top, it will cascade back down to the ground like a waterfall.

Hyacinth Bean
Dolichos lablab Syn.
Lablab purpureus

As mentioned earlier, this vine starts to flower in midsummer. The flowers are lightly fragrant and a large cluster brought into a room gives a soft, light aroma. Usually the fragrance is just enough to notice but not enough to draw undo interest like a gardenia flower. While the flower of the straight species is purple, a white version named 'Albus' is available, as well as a bicolored pink flower called 'Ruby Moon'. The flowers will continue to produce throughout the summer and into fall. As cooler nights approach, flower production will taper off, and by the time the first killing frost arrives, only pods will be left on the vine. Fortunately, they are so attractive that they have ornamental value by themselves. The pods are often 4–6 inches long and are a deep purple that blends well with the dark green leaves.

We have seen Hyacinth Bean used as an arbor vine as well as a specimen planting with its own support from a metal pole or trellis. Both uses work equally well. This vine needs full sun and will give less than satisfactory results if treated otherwise. Gardeners who insist that morning sun is sufficient will be disappointed. Although Hyacinth Bean is attractive up close, it does not look its best in small, enclosed spaces. Instead, use this plant where you can admire it from a distance or along a path. As long as full sun is abundant and strong support such as a fence, arbor, or trellis is available, you will not be disappointed.

Climbing method: twining stems • Sun: full sun • Moisture: needs regular watering • Hardiness Zone: 9–10 • Heat Zone: 6–11 • Propagation: seeds. Soaking the seeds overnight is recommended. Pods with the seeds in them can be collected and stored in a cool dry place until spring

Hyacinth Bean
Dolichos lablab Syn.
Lablab purpureus

Moonvine
Ipomoea alba
The Moonvine is probably Brian's favorite annual vine. In fact, it's the only annual vine he plants in his garden every year. Two things about this vine make it different from other annual vines. First, it has very large white flowers, and second, the plant blooms at night. The average flower is about 6 inches across and this gargantuan size allows the Moonvine to make a bold visual statement from several yards away. The Moonvine in Brian's garden is always on a front porch post, and is easily visible from the street, which is about 40–50 feet away. P.J. lets hers ramble along a tall fence that runs perpendicular to a busy thoroughfare. Passersby get a glimpse of it as they approach a neighbor's drive.

Moonvine
Ipomoea alba

Moonvine also offers up a wonderful soft fragrance when its flowers open around sunset or early evening. This affords folks who work during the day the opportunity to enjoy their gardens after coming home. Although each flower lasts but one night, the vine produces copious blossoms beginning in midsummer. For those who like to bring fragrant flowers into the house, place some of these spiral-shaped buds in a vase or bowl of water during the late afternoon. When the flowers open, they will scent the room.

Moonvine, like most annual vines, can be used in many different ways. Because of the night-blooming fragrant flowers, it is best used in an area that is frequented by the gardener, such as a deck or a post by the doorway.

Moonvine
Ipomoea alba

Climbing method: twining stems • Sun: full sun • Moisture: tolerates drought, although flowering will be reduced • Hardiness Zone: 9–10 • Heat Zone: 6–11 • Propagation: seeds. Germination is poor; soaking the seeds overnight is really necessary. One plant produces many seeds, and seedlings will readily come up the next spring

Morning Glory

Ipomoea tricolor

The morning glory is an annual vine that has a history of being despised. In recent years, however, gardeners have discovered the ornamental virtues of this once-hated weed. The morning glory vine has the ability to grow very rapidly and produce numerous seeds that will generate hundreds of plants the following year. These characteristics make it attractive to gardeners, as well as to growers who produce these plants for the market. However, if you are trying to till a couple of hundred acres of food crops, the ability of the morning glory to grow and reproduce is not seen with kind affection.

What grandeur they can display! Few plants have the ability to match the flower power of morning glories during the post-dawn hours. Throughout

Morning Glory
Ipomoea tricolor

the night, the flowers begin to surge from their buds. Then, as the sun appears over the horizon, they start to open. Because there is almost no nighttime evaporation, the plant can replace its daylight hours' water depletion, thereby allowing the flowers to expand to their maximum blooming capacity. Although dazzling, the flowers last for only a short time. One who is prone to sleeping in should not expect to see the benefits of a morning glory vine. Brian remembers a quote from the garden writer Reginald Arkell: "If you don't look at them before breakfast, you probably don't see them it all." We frequently witness the truth of Mr. Arkell's statement and find the paradox perplexing. Here is a plant, native to Mexico and South America, whose only requirements for growth are heat and moisture. However, its flowers are so dainty and delicate that they can withstand only the first gentle hours of sunlight before collapsing into a shriveled mess. We must admit that the beauty of each flower will stop us in our tracks and cause us to stand there, admiring each bloom individually before moving on down the path.

Morning Glory is a vigorous grower and can easily cover an arbor in a month or two if given ample moisture. Because the seeds are produced in such great number and germinate so easily, it is best to use this vine where it has lots of room to cover. The flowers can be enjoyed from a distance. In a garden setting, volunteer seedlings can be kept in check with a modest amount of diligence. Numerous species of morning glory exist, including many hybrids. Flower colors range from blue to red and everything in between.

Climbing method: twining stems • Sun: full sun • Moisture: needs regular watering • Hardiness Zone: 9–10 • Heat Zone: 1–12 • Propagation: seeds. Soaking the seeds overnight is recommended. One plant produces many seeds, and seedlings will readily come up the next spring.

Morning Glories

As a youngster growing up on a farm in upstate South Carolina, I remember the disgust my father had for morning glories because they were a constant nuisance in our crops. I must admit that my prejudice for this plant, instilled in me by the culture of eking a living from the soil, made it difficult for me to accept it as a desirable ornamental. My warming up to morning glories is owed to the excellent skills of horticulturists, who not only pointed out the virtues of this plant, but enlightened me to its beauty as an ornamental vine. (I have not had the courage to attempt this with my father, though.) Don't misunderstand me. My family did notice the flowers each morning as we went into the fields, and we did have moments of appreciation for their beauty. However, that good feeling was quickly displaced whenever we were forced to exert great effort and resources to remove it from our growing crops where it competed for the ever-precious water in the dry summer soil. Now, as I no longer must fight the elements *per se* to earn a living, I can appreciate the beauty of a summer morning with the dew still fresh on the grass and the morning glory flowers displaying their grandeur.

I still can't bring myself to use this plant in my own garden. I enjoy it only when visiting someone else's garden. Some prejudices die hard. I am happy for any gardener who can enjoy this vine and use it in his or her garden, especially if I get the privilege of visiting it from time to time to admire the flowers.

Brian

Cardinal Vine

Ipomoea × multifida

This vine is a hybrid between *I. coccineus* (Red Morning Glory) and *I. quamo-clit* (Cypress Vine), and Brian simply loves the vase-shaped bright red flowers. They are very showy, with tubular necks that flare into pentagonal stars. The flowers alone are enough to hold even the most begrudging observer. However, the foliage, which resembles a palm-like leaf with long reaching "fingers," is also dramatic. The combination of the wonderful flowers and the attractive foliage is spectacular. This plant can be used in a container, on an arbor, along a fence, espaliered along a wall, or allowed to grow over a rounded structure, giving it a mounded growth habit. It is also a plant that just loves hot and humid weather. That's because one of its parents, the Cypress Vine, is native to the American tropics. Although many home gardeners assume that native plants are always well behaved, Cypress Vine is a truly invasive, weedy vine. In spite of its beautiful flowers, *I. quamoclit* should be avoided unless one is willing to expend continual effort removing unwanted seedlings. Make certain the plant you're purchasing has the botanical name on the label. Cypress Vine is sometimes called "Cardinal Climber." The similarity of the common names could cause you to purchase the wrong plant.

It is our good fortune that the Cardinal Vine did not inherit a weedy nature from its other parent, *I. coccineus*. The blending of each parent's "good" genes results in a fantastic annual vine that tolerates everything that hot and humid weather can throw at it, while producing a never-ending flow of red flowers from midsummer until the first frost.

While *Ipomoea × multifida* is not a weedy pest like one of its parents, this plant, as with any member of the *Ipomoea* genus, easily reproduces from seed. Expect some rogue and therefore undesirable seedlings. However, it lacks both parents' fecundity. Growing one is certainly worth the effort.

Climbing method: twining stems • Sun: full sun • Moisture: needs regular watering • Hardiness Zone: 9–10 • Heat Zone: 1–12 • Propagation: To aid germination, seeds should be scarified (slice part of the outer seed coat) and soaked in water for 12–24 hours

Mandevilla
Mandevilla spp.

Mandevillas are popular in the south and are therefore abundantly available. These vines will add a tropical look to your garden. The large showy flowers appear in clusters of three to four with long tunnel-like tubes with a broad opening. Depending on the cultivar, you may chose from pink, white, or yellow-throated ones. The white dipladenia (*M. boliviensis*) has an orange-yellow throat. All of the Mandevillas' relatively large leaves have pinnate or feather-like veination. This gives them a coarse look that adds to the foliage's aesthetic appeal.

According to horticultural literature, some species are slightly fragrant. However, it has been our experience that the commonly available ones have no detectable smell unless you're willing to bury your nose in the flower and take a very deep breath. One species that does have a significant fragrance is *M. laxa* (Chilean jasmine). Allan Armitage lists it in his book *Manual of Annuals, Biennials, and Half-Hardy Perennials* as the most fragrant of the Mandevillas available to gardeners.

The challenge to growing Mandevillas is their stubbornness to respond in cool climates. Being native of tropical South America, Mandevillas aren't inclined to cooperate during our spring and fall temperatures. So, if you live in an area where the summer is relatively short, coaxing it to flower can be a problem. And they simply refuse to bloom until the plant has reached maturity. In these situations, you must therefore start it in the greenhouse while the nighttime temperatures are still below 40° F. Then, once the temperatures warm up, move it outside. After Mandevilla starts to flower, it will continue to do so until the nighttime temperatures return to 40° F.

We recommend using Mandevillas where you can get that midsummer tropical look. (We are partial to the large pink flowers.) Mandevillas should be easy to find in southern gardening centers and, as tropical plants go, they are not expensive.

Climbing method: twining stems • Sun: full sun • Moisture: needs regular watering • Hardiness Zone: 9–10, sometimes 8 • Heat Zone: 1–12 • Propagation: softwood cuttings 3–4 inches long or seeds

Yellow Orchid Vine, Butterfly Vine

Mascagnia macroptera

Very little has been written about this vine and we eagerly await the day when someone decides to make an in-depth study of this plant. The Yellow Orchid Vine is an evergreen and native to Baja California in Mexico. It is used in the arid west as an ornamental because, once it is established, it has excellent drought tolerance. However, little information is known about its performance in humid regions; there are intimations that suggest it adapts to our type of climate quite well. We have unsubstantiated reports that folks in Baton Rouge (USDA Hardiness Zone 8b) are successfully growing these vines.

We are eager to learn more about this plant. The vine grows to about 15 feet in length and, during the summer, it produces an abundance of yellow orchid-like flowers, hence one of its common names. The chartreuse fruit pods that form during late summer are butterfly-shaped, hence that common name. (But does it attract butterflies? We don't know.) The leaves are dark green and offer a stunning contrast against the flowers. The vine is a perennial in Zones 8b and higher. It will come back from the roots if hit by frost and can withstand 25° F before the roots are killed.

Mascagnia macroptera can also be allowed to grow into a shrub-like form because of its propensity to twine on itself. The self-twining will result in a mound about 3–4 feet tall and 5–6 feet wide and it will continue to spread as a ground cover. Although its drought tolerance makes this plant highly desirable, we have been told that it looks much nicer if it is watered regularly.

If you are ever strolling through a garden center and see this vine offered, grab it. Take a chance on this vine in your garden because the exotic orchid-like flowers are worth the effort.

Climbing method: twining stems • Sun: full sun • Moisture: moderate watering until established, drought-tolerant after establishment • Hardiness Zone: 8–10 • Heat Zone: 5–12 (estimated) • Propagation: seeds and cuttings

Passionflower

Passiflora spp.

Many native southerners' first recollection of Passionflower is the old reliable Maypop (*P. incarnata*), a common, slightly weedy vine that's native to the south. For most of Brian's adult gardening life, he looked upon Passionflower as pretty flowers growing on scraggly weedy vines. P.J. thought the flowers were garish. They looked too much like plastic five-and-dime plants. The Passionflower fruit seems to frighten a lot of Yankees. They are always asking us if they are poisonous. (Their reasoning: a plant that flamboyant has to be dangerous.) But over the past couple of years, we have come to appreciate the abundance of species and varieties of Passionflower available to the gardener. According to Dr. Allan Armitage, over five hundred species of *Passiflora* have

Passionflower
Passiflora spp.

been identified, with numerous varieties inside several of those species. So if you're stuck with one image of Passionflower—white and purple flowers, we are happy to announce that there are colors as diverse as bright red, yellow, and bluish pink.

Almost all Passionflower species have fragrant flowers. 'Elizabeth' and 'Incense' are quite aromatic. Of course, most people familiar with Passionflower think of their attractiveness to butterflies. Several butterfly species use the Passionflower as a food source for the larva.

Growing Passionflowers is very simple. You will have good success with them if you offer full sun and modest amounts of fertilizer. Over-fertilization will lead to the vines' producing an abundance of foliage and almost no flowers. The other thing to consider is temperature.

Some forms are very tolerant of our cool springs. Others, however, especially the tropical forms, will not perform well if they are planted outside in cool weather. For the northern gardener, these types may not flower at all. It is also important to know whether you have a hardy, semi-hardy, or tropical form. The hardy forms can be treated as perennials in Zones 7 and 8. The semi-hardy forms defoliate at temperatures below 40° F and perform best when maintained at temperatures of 45–50° F. The tropical forms must stay at temperatures above 50° F to do well.

The name Passionflower comes from early missionaries who saw the flower parts as a semblance of Christ's crucifixion. Of course, the most obvious metaphor is the corona, which symbolizes the crown of thorns.

For the complete rundown on Passionflowers, read John Vanderplank's *Passion Flowers.*

Climbing method: tendrils • Sun: full sun • Moisture: needs regular watering • Hardiness Zone: depends on species • Heat Zone: depends on species • Propagation: softwood cuttings in midsummer or seeds

Passiflora

I clearly recall walking down the rows of sweet corn in late summer, harvesting the ears we had grown on our farm. (For the non-agricultural gardener, sweet corn must be harvested by hand. No machine can tell if an ear of sweet corn is ready to be picked. Field corn can be mechanically harvested because the ears of corn have been allowed to completely dry out before they are picked.) As we walked down the towering rows of corn, the Maypop fruits would "pop" under our feet. Even as a child, trained only in the ways of growing food, I could not help but admire and enjoy looking at the Maypop flowers. The vines did not appeal to me that much but the flowers would hold my gaze, at least until Daddy caught me "goofing off" and verbally chastised me for not picking corn (a charge with some merit).

Brian

Scarlet Runner Bean, Jefferson Plant

Phaseolus coccineus

This native of Central America's mountain valleys is often used in Florida gardens as an ornamental. Scarlet Runner Bean has dark green foliage with a tinge of purple on the underside along the veins. It will reach 15–20 feet in length during one season and only needs something close to it to scurry up. A University of Florida publication comments on its fondness for television towers. The dark foliage serves as an excellent backdrop to the bright red flowers that appear in the middle of summer. With about twenty blossoms per cluster, the vine produces a semi-showy bloom of scarlet red flowers spaced along the panicle. The seedpods are edible and reasonably palatable, although rather stringy.

The Scarlet Runner Bean can obviously serve double duty as a beautiful ornamental vine and a good vegetable plant. It is also an attractant for butterflies and hummingbirds, offering both sweet nectar. When you stop and think about it, the Scarlet Runner Bean is a wise choice for the gardener with limited space. It has ornamental value, attracts wildlife, and is a source of fresh vegetables. If offered a pole or some other small area structure, this plant will take up little space in an already small area. Not many plants can do all that for a gardener. However, there is one catch. (We assume that you suspected this was coming. Otherwise, this would be the perfect plant.) Do you remember the native habitat we mentioned earlier? Growing in the tropical mountain valleys, the pollen is not viable once temperatures reach 90° F or higher. So, while we will still get plenty of flowers during the hot summer months, the fruit pods will not set until the temperatures cool down again at the beginning of fall. Fortunately, this problem only affects the fruit, but don't plan on serving up any pods in July or August.

From our perspective, Scarlet Runner Bean can be used in any form or style a *Some Like It Hot* gardener chooses. Being a traditionalist, however, Brian thinks it belongs on a fence or pole like any other respectable climbing vegetable. Still, it would make a striking display on any arbor, and this vine deserves more than being relegated to a beanpole.

Climbing method: twining stems • Sun: full sun to partial shade • Moisture: needs regular watering • Hardiness Zone: 9–10, sometimes 8 • Heat Zone: 1–12 (estimated) • Propagation: seeds

Mexican Flame Vine

Pseudogynoxys chenopodioides Syn. *Senecio confuses*

This native of tropical Mexico is a great performer when it receives morning sun and afternoon shade (it can take full sun in Zones 4, 5, and 6). It is a member of the daisy family, so its bright orange flowers look just like the rest of its cousins. These attractive orange blossoms are the reason for one of its common names, Orange-Glow Vine. Mexican Flame Vine was once called *Senecio confuses* until taxonomists recently renamed it.

Mexican Flame Vine offers gardeners good growth, appealing orange flowers, *and* it is pest-resistant. However, you are going to have to give it plenty of water. Another quality of Mexican Flame Vine is its ability to grow on a structure or to spread out as a ground cover. It's up to the gardener to determine its ultimate growth habit. The vine's ability to flower is not compromised by how you decide to grow it. It will also flower well with only a half-day's sun exposure. This makes it a good container plant for piazzas and porches.

Climbing method: twining stems • Sun: half-day sun • Moisture: needs regular watering • Hardiness Zone: 9–10 • Heat Zone: 5–12 (estimated) • Propagation: seeds or cuttings

Black-Eyed Susan Vine

Thunbergia alata

Black-Eyed Susan Vine simply begs to be used in a basket or container. It has triangular green leaves that are 2–3 inches long, which makes it an ideal contrast plant. The vine will almost instantly start growing down to the ground from the edges of the container, which eventually creates a cascading waterfall appearance. The yellow to orange flowers shortly follow. They will open up to an inch or so wide and will be 2 inches long. In the center of each one will be a dark throat, which gives it the "black-eyed" look it gets its name from.

It is a native of tropical east Africa, so this vine quickly adapts to the heat and humidity of our summers. The wonderful thing about this plant is its quick out-of-the-gate growth spurt in the spring. If you live in Zones 9 or greater, Black-Eyed Susan Vine will be a returning perennial for you. If you put it in protected areas of Zone 8b, it will act as a perennial as well. Even in all the other zones, where it behaves as an annual, you can have this plant up and leafing out as soon as the last threat of frost passes in the spring. Because it is a fast grower, this vine will quickly cover a pole or short trellis and be blooming by early summer. While it has a moderate to heavy water requirement, it has no pest problems to speak of.

For the novice gardener learning to work with annual plants, Black-Eyed Susan Vine is a good confidence-builder. For the busy gardener who does not have time to pamper plants, this is a great plant to get started in the spring, offer it support with a moderate amount of training, and then enjoy the flower show at your leisure. All it requires is a lot of water.

Climbing method: twining stems • Sun: full to partial sun • Moisture: needs regular watering • Hardiness Zone: 9–10, sometimes 8 • Heat Zone: 5–12 • Propagation: seeds sown in the soil after danger of frost has passed, or start in flats. Soak the seeds overnight before planting.

Blue Sky Vine, Blue Indian Vine
Thunbergia grandiflora

Here is a vine that is worthy of everyone's garden. Why would we make such a bold, presumptuous statement? Because this *Thunbergia grandiflora* is a late-summer bloomer! Beginning in July or August, this vine produces huge blue flowers with yellow or white throats. By now, all the other annual vines have been blooming for at least several weeks. In fact, you're probably beginning to take those vines for granted. But just when you've grudgingly adjusted to a somewhat boring landscape at the height of the dog days of summer, *bam!* Out pop these brilliant blue flowers.

A native of tropical India, Blue Sky Vine grows 50 feet long in its homeland. However, for us in the more temperate climes, it will reach only 15–30 feet, depending on how many frost-free days you have. The 6–8 inch coarse-textured, succulent leaves will also grab your attention. This visual interest is important because it takes so long for the vine to flower. It is a robust climber, so it needs a strong support. Put a wire a structure at the end of the support so it can spread out and flow back toward the ground. When fully open, the flowers are about 3 inches long with a 2-inch width. The mauve blue color is simply stunning.

While almost any plant benefits from soil amendments, Blue Sky Vine truly depends on them. It is a heavy feeder, so you really need to add those supplements before planting. It needs a rich humus soil to grow well in. It is also a plant that will need regular watering. In fact, you should not grow this plant if you're not prepared to provide it regular water. You won't need a bog garden to grow it in—just put it in a spot where running a hose to it for extra water is not a hassle. You should also plant this vine in full sun. Don't waste your time planting it in partial shade.

Cold hardiness is hard to nail down with this plant. According to some very reliable literature, it is only a perennial in USDA Zone 9. However, these plants have returned several years in a row at the herbaceous trail gardens at the University of Georgia (USDA Zone 7).

Climbing method: twining stems • Sun: full sun • Moisture: needs regular watering • Hardiness Zone: 9–10 (7–10 in some literature) • Heat Zone: 5–12 • Propagation: seeds or cuttings

Orange Clock Vine
Thunbergia gregorii

For all practical purposes, we could have just said "See *Thunbergia alata*" for the scoop on Orange Clock Vine. They are similar in every aspect except for some taxonomical features. The growth habits and culture are also the same. What makes this species different are the flowers. They are slightly larger than those of the Black-Eyed Susan Vine, and are burnt orange with no "eye." They are truly a mesmerizing flower when seen for the first time. Brian has grown this vine for several years at his home (USDA Zone 8b) and it has always come back from the roots like a perennial. He loves this vine because of the cascading effect that is common to all the *Thunbergias*. He uses it on the back side of a short brick wall. It grows up a small wooden ladder to the top of the wall then grows down the front side. This gives the effect of a waterfall cascading down the front wall. The vine pops out with new growth at the first hint of spring, and grows rapidly, so by the time the buds are starting to form, the vines are already spilling over. Don't you just love it when something works out that perfectly?

Climbing method: twining stems • Sun: full sun • Moisture: needs regular watering • Hardiness Zone: 9–10, sometimes 8 in protected areas • Heat Zone: 5–12 • Propagation: cuttings or seed

Orange Clock Vine
Thunbergia greggori

Snail Vine, Caracalla Bean
Vigna caracalla Syn. *Phaseolus caracalla*

This is another vine about which we have scant information. In fact, here is what all the great minds in horticulture have to say about this plant: It is native to tropical America, it can reach 20 feet in length, and it has "curious fragrant blue flowers." We have found only one method of propagation, which is by seed. The common name Snail Vine comes from the flower having a snail-like appearance. The flower is curled around itself just like a snail in the shell. They start out a soft baby blue, but as they begin to age, they turn a deeper blue, then finally a light yellow, before completely fading away. This colorful display is truly outstanding and this trait is quite uncommon among annuals.

The flowers are unbelievably fragrant. They are reminiscent of tea olives. If you are unfamiliar with tea olives, then imagine a gardenia flower that does not overpower you to the point of being sickening like a bottle of cheap, spilled perfume. The scent of the Snail Vine flower is gently sweet without being too sticky. The fragrance will easily scent a small area outdoors. While we have never tried this, we suspect an inflorescence brought indoors and placed in a vase would easily fill a room with the sweet soft smell of the Snail Vine.

Brian knows of only one person who has extensively used this vine. Hunter Stubbs, the horticulturist at Richmond Hill Inn in Asheville, NC, grows this vine each year as part of his summer annuals program. Hunter starts the seeds each spring and then

Snail Vine
Vigna caracalla

transplants them outside after the danger of frost has passed. He also keeps a three-year-old plant as a back-up. This assures him that he'll have seeds for the next season if something goes wrong with the new vines. He digs up the "mother" each fall and places it in a container until the following spring. Hunter's Snail Vines produce flowers by the middle of July in Asheville. Not an easy feat for annual vines that live in the cool mountain air of North Carolina.

Climbing method: twining stems • Sun: full sun • Moisture: needs regular watering • Hardiness Zone: 8–10 • Heat Zone: 5–12 (estimated)

Snail Vine
Vigna caracalla

Propagation: *Some Like It Hot* Annual Vine Seed Planting Guide

Plant Name	Days to germination	Slow or irregular germination	Temperature to germinate	Seed depth	Comments
Antigonon leptopus Coral Vine	21–30		65–70°	Just cover the seed with potting soil.	
Aristolochia spp. Calico Flower Dutchman's Pipe	30–90	Yes	75–80°	Sow on the surface but do not cover.	Needs light to germinate. Hot soak 48 hrs.
Clerodendrum splendens Bleeding Heart Vine	21–60	Yes	70–75°	$1/8''$	
Clitoria ternatea Blue Snails Vine	15–20		70–75°	$1/6''$	Nick and then soak 24 hrs.
Cobaea scandens Cup-and-Saucer Vine	21–30	Seeds are often difficult to germinate.	65–85°	$1/6''$	Soak overnight. Stick seeds vertically in soil.
Dicentra scandens Yellow Bleeding Heart Vine	30–180	Yes	55–60°	Just cover the seed with potting soil.	Needs light to germinate.
Dolichos lablab Hyacinth Bean, Lablab	14–30		70°	$1/16''$	Soak for 24 hrs.
Ipomoea spp. Moonvine, Morning Glory, Cardinal Vine	5–21	Yes	70–85°	$1/4''$	Nick and then soak for 24 hrs.

Propagation: *Some Like It Hot* Annual Vine Seed Planting Guide (continued)

Plant Name	Days to germination	Slow or irregular germination	Temperature to germinate	Seed depth	Comments
Mandevilla spp. Mandevilla	14–30		65–70°	Just cover the seed with potting soil.	Sow in half sand/half potting soil.
Passiflora spp. Passionflower	30–365	Yes. Erratic germination	70–85°	1/4"	Soak for 24 hrs. Sow, then pre-chill for 3 months. Give seed container an occasional soak.
Phaseolus coccineus Scarlet Runner Bean, Jefferson Plant	30–60		60–70°	1/16"	Nick and then soak for 24 hrs.
Pseudogynoxys chenopodioides Syn. *Senecio confusus* Mexican Flame Vine	10–21		65–75°	1/16"	Needs light to germinate.
Thunbergia spp. Black-Eyed Susan Vine, Blue Sky Vine, Blue Indian Vine, Orange Clock Vine	14–21	Yes	70–75°	Just cover the seed with potting soil.	Keep soil slightly moist (Soak *T. alata* seeds overnight.)
Vigna caracalla Snail Vine, Caracalla Bean	14–30		65–85°	1/6"	Nick and then soak for 24 hrs.

Small Shrubs

It has been our experience that too many of us plant the wrong shrub in the wrong place. Why is it that, while no one would ever dream of trying to stuff a cello into a violin case, we cheerfully shove shrubs into too-small spaces and then sulk when they don't meet our expectations?

Our own personal gardening blunders have taught us that, unless a person considers a shrub's eventual mature size *before* planting, it will probably end up being stuck in the wrong place. And chances are that incorrect spot was way too small for your shrub. Fortunately, small shrubs are the munchkins of woody ornamentals and only reach about three feet tall at maturity. These little buddies hardly ever encounter a space that's too small for them.

We have divided shrub sizes into four categories:

Small shrubs	3 feet or less at maturity
Small to medium shrubs	3-6 feet at maturity
Medium to large shrubs	Over 6 feet tall at maturity
Large shrubs and small/patio trees	Tree status at maturity

Small shrubs should be most people's first choice for those much-needed foundation plantings around a house. This is because most of these beds are very narrow (and in many cases, disproportionately so). Another important consideration is view. Plants often block windows after they get over three feet tall. Once the height between the ground and windows is considered, as well as the narrow bed width from the house to the lawn, it becomes apparent that a plant grown under such limited circumstances should be no more than three feet tall and just as wide.

The plants we have listed in our *Some Like It Hot* small shrub section will meet your limited space needs, yet provide your garden with some color during the hottest time of summer. They will also provide you with all the features you expect in foundation plantings. Furthermore, small shrubs are usually incapable of becoming a later nuisance around windows, water spigots, and vents.

You'll discover other areas that cry out for larger plants. In the long run, you're actually getting more plants than you would have otherwise. After all, you can only have so many azaleas in your landscape. If you put them all around the foundation, then you are severely limiting your plant selection. By using small shrubs around your house and placing those prized azaleas elsewhere, you have added more diversity to your horticultural environment.

Some Like It Hot Small Shrubs	
Ardisia crenata	Coralberry
A. japonica	Japanese Ardisia, Marlberry
Aronia melanocarpa	Black Chokeberry
Gardenia augusta 'Radicans' (formerly *G. jasminodes* 'Radicans')	Dwarf Gardenia
Indigofera decora	Pink Indigo
Lagerstroemia hybrids	Dwarf Crepe Myrtles

Coralberry

Ardisia crenata

A very cold-sensitive brother of Japanese Ardisia, Coralberry is probably the more aesthetically appealing of the two. The leaves are a lustrous dark green and the edges, or leaf margins, are crenated. This gives a softer appearance than its sharply serrated relative does. The best word picture we can use for someone who has never seen Coralberry is Awabuki Viburnum (*V. awabuki*). Imagine an Awabuki Viburnum with bright red fruit the size of a grape. Coralberry has the same glossy, shiny leaves and similar leaf margins. The leaf's overall size and shape are much like Japanese Viburnum but Coralberry's slightly larger flowers will have some pink. The Coralberry will also bear bigger fruit.

Coralberry will reach heights of 2–4 feet in mild, frost-free climates. In Zones 6 and 7, it will be killed back to the roots. Like Japanese Ardisia, Coralberry will bear white to pink flowers in July and August and bright red fruit that will persist into winter. The fruit stays around much longer than Japanese Ardisia's, thus providing landscape interest throughout the winter. 'Alba' is a white-fruited form for gardeners with a desire for white berries.

Like its brother, Coralberry does best in some shade. Many plant experts suggest never growing it in full sun because of foliage burn risks. Planting

Coralberry
Ardisia crenata

Coralberry in the shade also offers it some winter protection. Cold injury often results when plant stems are exposed to direct full sun on a cold winter's morning when temperatures are at or below freezing. The sun causes the stem tissue to rapidly warm up, which results in vascular tissue damage, which leads to the plant's death. Cold-sensitive plants growing on the north side of a house, or in shaded areas, do not often experience bark splitting along the trunk and stems. When protected stem tissues are allowed to warm up gradually, they are less likely to rupture. A word of caution to gardeners in frost-free areas: Coralberry has become an invasive plant in some parts of Florida. Before you use it, check with a local horticulturist to make sure you want to include it in your landscape.

Once you get to know it, Coralberry is a plant that you'll really start to like. Its affinity for the shade makes it a valuable plant to use when you want color (i.e., flowers or berries) at various times of the year, but lack full sun.

Height: 2–4 feet • Spread: 2–4 feet • Sun: partial shade to shade, avoid full sun • Moisture: regular moisture until established, then can tolerate short periods of drought • Hardiness Zone: 8–9; will be killed back to the roots in Zones 6 and 7 • Heat Zone: 7–11 (estimated) • Propagation: stem cuttings

Japanese Ardisia, Marlberry

Ardisia japonica

Japanese Ardisia, sometimes called Marlberry, may well be a plant that should be categorized as a groundcover. Nonetheless, we include it with small shrubs because of its "shrubby" potential. The only thing that will limit the appeal and use of this excellent small shrub/groundcover is its absence of the cold-hardiness trait. Japanese Ardisia has demonstrated a propensity to succumb to those infrequent yet cruel cold winter nights that unfortunately beset *Some Like It Hot* gardens. Dr. Michael Dirr, in his book titled *Manual of Woody Landscape Plants*, notes that his Japanese Ardisia was completely killed in his Athens, Georgia, garden when temperatures dropped to 7° and 19° F. While the cold-hardiness rating for Japanese Ardisia is listed for USDA Zones 5 and 6, it is best to look at this plant as viable in Zones 7–9.

As for its ability to tolerate heat and humidity, Japanese Ardisia can hold its own throughout the dog days of summer. While we have not seen it used extensively, we have never come across a plant that was rampant with heat-related diseases or humid summer infirmities. Because it is native to Japan and China (the name "japonica" should clue you to that), Japanese Ardisia is very accustomed to humidity and warm temperatures. However, it does have an aversion to a lot of direct sunlight, although it performs well in shade.

If you can overcome its cold-hardiness problem, we're confident that you'll quickly develop an affection for this plant—especially if you have a shady spot where you need a low-growing shrub or groundcover. In most cases, the plant will grow to 12 inches tall, but can reach up to 18 inches in some situations. The evergreen leaves are whorled at the end of the petiole. The sharply serrated leaf margins give them a texture that has been described by some as bold and resembling Hellebores. The flowers appear in July to August as white to pale pink stars on long racemes. While the flowers will certainly catch your attention during midsummer, the bright red berries that form in September and October make a stronger statement. Expect them to remain until winter unless confiscated by the local wildlife.

Many variegated forms and cultivars have found their way onto garden center shelves and we would be remiss if we didn't mention them. While varieties like 'Beniyuki' and 'Chiyoda' will provide the standard white variegation around the leaf edges, 'Amanogawa' has a splash of gold in the center of the leaf. 'Nishiki' has gold and pink variegated leaves; the new leaves start out with pink variegation then turn to a golden yellow color as they age.

We don't want to leave you with the impression that Japanese Ardisia is without aesthetic appeal for the remainder of the year. The dark green leaves and thick cover provide a nice sea of green in a semi-shady garden spot. Brian believes the best use for this plant is under that large shade tree where turf won't grow, but another liriope bed won't offer enough color. If you are one of the fortunate *Some Like It Hot* gardeners who can use this plant without fretting over losing it on a cold winter's night, then *Ardisia japonica* is a plant you definitely should investigate and add to your less-than-full-sun repertoire.

Height: 12 inches • Spread: spreads by rhizomes • Sun: avoid full sun; partial to full shade is best • Moisture: regular moisture during establishment, then short periods of drought can be tolerated • Hardiness Zone: 7–9, best in 8–9, can be used in Zones 5 or 6 if right site is used with careful cultivar selection • Heat Zone: 7–11 (estimated) • Propagation: division of rhizomes

Black Chokeberry

Aronia melanocarpa

Black Chokeberry is a plant that is most useful to the "cooler" *Some Like It Hot* gardeners. Although native from Nova Scotia to Florida, and as far west as Michigan, this plant is really more viable for folks in ASHS heat Zones 1–10. While it may do well in Heat Zones 11 and 12 under the right conditions, it might get too temperamental.

Although Black Chokeberry can grow to 10–12 feet, it usually reaches only 3–5 feet. The flowers are not very showy when they appear in April or May (or even as early as March in some warmer climates). The aesthetic impact comes from the black to purplish berries that appear in May and last through September. They offer a nice feature and, when this plant is used in massive plantings, the berries really make a bold statement. With age, the plant will probably develop a very heavy fruit set, making a truly spectacular show. In many zones, the berry-laden plants will offer wine-red leaves in the fall. Of course, this added benefit is fall foliage color and black berries at the same time.

To us, though, Black Chokeberry's most attractive feature is not an aesthetic one. This plant likes wet soil! Although it also adapts to well-drained soils if provided with regular watering, chokeberry is an excellent choice for wetland areas. If you are one of those poor souls who must struggle with a soggy area in your garden most of the year, then you know how difficult it is to find appropriate plants. This plant, like many others that are well adapted to wet soils, will eventually create spreading colonies with rhizomes and suckering. It will easily fill in those voids in your private little swamp.

One drawback to Black Chokeberry is that it tends to get leggy and gangly. This is especially true with the straight species. Fortunately, several varieties are available that offer better characteristics for the home landscape. Dr. Dirr considers 'Elata' a superior variety. Others with good characteristics are 'Autumn Magic', which is more compact, and 'Iroquois Beauty', which is a dwarf form staying 2–3 feet tall.

Height: 3–5 feet, sometimes more • Spread: 3–5 feet • Sun: full sun or shade, but more fruit in full sun • Moisture: likes wet soils, but does well in other soils if watered regularly • Hardiness Zone: 3–9 • Heat Zone: 1–10 • Propagation: easily roots from softwood cuttings in midsummer. Division of colonies is also a good method

Dwarf Gardenia
Gardenia augusta 'Radicans'
(formerly *G. jasminodes* 'Radicans')
Gardenias have long been a garden staple in hot and humid climates, so much so that they are ubiquitous in the south. (P.J.'s standard Master Gardener response to anyone who asks about planting them is, "You want to do *what*?") You either love 'em or hate 'em. At the expense of restating the already-known to most southern gardeners, let's review this familiar plant.

The Dwarf Gardenia is very similar to its larger relative, *G. augusta* (formerly *G. jasminodes*). The leaves have the same dark green color but the Dwarf

Gardenia's are lance-shaped and significantly smaller. The regular or common gardenia will grow to 4–6 feet tall, but the dwarf reaches only 2–3 feet. The smaller version spreads to about 4 feet, making it look like a mounded shrub. Its white flowers are wonderfully fragrant when they open in midsummer. They lack that sticky-sweet, cheap-perfume smell that is so characteristic of the common gardenia. (We find the odoriferous effect of the common gardenia akin to motion sickness.) However, the Dwarf Gardenia's bouquet is quite pleasant.

Dwarf Gardenia
Gardenia augusta
'Radicans'

A Conversation with Ted Stephens about Gardenias

On the issue of gardenias and winter injury, I remember a conversation I had one day with the great plant guru Ted Stephens, co-owner of Nurseries Caroliniana in North Augusta, South Carolina. Ted told me that Fred Thode, former professor of horticulture at Clemson University, always insisted that gardenias should be planted on the north side of a house. The absence of warm winter sunlight falling on them would prevent most cold injury. Consequently, the sun-protected gardenias would always look better than the ones exposed to the winter sun.

Since that landmark day in my development as a horticulturist, I have been a keen observer of gardenias to see if Professor Thode's advice via Ted was true. I can say emphatically that his admonition was valid. Keep the sun off your gardenias in the winter! They will perform better because they will have less or no winter injury.

Brian

A variety called 'Radicans Variegata' offers the same characteristics as the 'Radicans' but with creamy white variegation along the leaf margins.

Gardenias are native to China and, while they are well adapted to humidity, they often suffer cold injury during the winter. Like the Coralberry, if gardenias are exposed to the sun on frosty or sub-freezing mornings, the sunlight hitting the plant will cause rapid warming and then rupture the vascular tissues. While it is true that gardenias, and this includes the Dwarf Gardenia, can grow in full sun, cold injury hurts more gardenias that have been planted in full sun than those growing in shade. Therefore, we recommend putting gardenias in the shade—or at least keep them away from early morning sun in the winter.

Of course, when veteran gardeners think of gardenias, the many pest challenges associated with them advance to the fore. Whiteflies are particularly

How the Gardenia Got Its Name

One of the cherished traditions in Charleston is naming buildings, sports complexes, or even highway overpasses after still-living community figures. Unfortunately, feelings can get hurt if one is repeatedly left off the nomination list. This is hardly a new situation. In 1755, then-Charleston resident Dr. Alexander Garden found himself in somewhat similar frustrating circumstances.

During the eighteenth century, having a plant named after oneself was considered among the highest forms of flattery. In fact, in some botanical circles, getting one's name approved for "a species of eternity" was an obsession. Never mind that the selection procedure was often scientifically and politically arduous, and quibbling sometimes threatened friendships. Such was the case with Dr. Garden's nomination.

People usually assume that the genus name *Gardenia* was awarded to this Scottish physician because he discovered the plant. And some folks think that Dr. Garden found the gardenia growing in Charleston. It's easy to understand the confusion because botanical names are often Latin derivatives of the discoverers' surnames. However, if that had been Dr. Carolus Linnaeus's unbreakable rule for botanical nomenclature, the gardenia should have been called "*Hutchinsonia.*"

During the 1740s, a Captain Hutchinson stopped at the Cape of Good Hope, "found" a gardenia, put it in a box and, upon returning to London, gave it to his friend, celebrated rare plant collector Richard Warner. Philip Miller, a renowned horticulturist and author of the *Gardener's Dictionary*, examined Warner's latest acquisition and declared it a Bay-Leaved Jasemin. He included it in his dictionary's next edition.

Meanwhile, across the Atlantic Ocean in Charleston, Dr. Garden was desperately trying to have his name officially associated with a plant—any plant. He had already been nominated twice, but Linnaeus, that supreme arbiter of plant classifications, had rejected both submissions.

In the meantime, John Ellis, an acclaimed naturalist and seed collector, and a close friend of both Linnaeus and Garden, stepped in to suggest several botanical names for Mr. Warner's plant after one of Linneaus's students discovered that it wasn't a jasmine but a new genus. Linnaeus kept holding out to name it *Warneria* (so much for Captain Hutchinson) but Warner refused the honor because he didn't want to offend Philip Miller. Never mind that Miller had misidentified the plant. Ellis grew increasingly impatient with Linnaeus because he thought his suggestions were being summarily dismissed. After a series of angry letters from Ellis, Linnaeus finally capitulated. "[M]y attachment to you will not easily permit me to go contrary to your determination."

The genus name *Gardenia* was finally awarded to Dr. Garden in the late autumn of 1760. After receiving the news, he wrote to Ellis saying, "I am wholly indebted to you for this high compliment…" The first gardenia in America arrived two years later in Charleston, compliments of Mr. Ellis.

troublesome. So much so, that some gardeners have completely given up on gardenias. Of course, with the whiteflies come sooty mold, that blackish fungus that colonizes on the honeydew excreted by the whiteflies. While the sooty mold poses no threat to the gardenias' overall health, it certainly distracts from their appearance. We offer no magic bullet. However, both of us have found that some gardenias have fewer whitefly problems than others. Could there be genetic factors involved, such as a resistant variety, or are cultural variables like a soil high in organic content important? We are unable to draw any firm conclusions.

Height: 2–3 feet • Spread: 4 feet, mounding often wider than higher • Sun: can take full sun, but will have less winter injury if planted in shade • Moisture: regular moisture, but drought-tolerant once established • Hardiness Zone: 7b–10 • Heat Zone: 3–11 • Propagation: softwood cuttings in midsummer

Pink Indigo

Indigofera decora

Pink Indigo has three characteristics that make it a great choice for *Some Like It Hot* gardens. First, the pink wisteria-like flowers begin to appear in late March and last into autumn. Anytime a woody plant blooms that long is reason enough to use it in your landscape. Its second attribute is that Pink Indigo, which is a smaller-growing form than many of its relatives, usually grows to only about 3 feet tall. Under certain conditions, it can grow an additional 12 inches, but that rarely happens. And finally, Pink Indigo is a shade plant. Although it will perform well in full sun in cooler climates, in most instances it should be grown in the shade. So, what Pink Indigo offers us is a rather small, compact shade plant that promises continual bloom during the dog days of summer.

When these three traits come bundled in one ornamental, everyone can come up with a reason to plant Pink Indigo. For example, that small shaded area in the niche between the steps and entrance wall often goes begging for color. Pink Indigo makes an excellent choice for this hard-to-fill gap.

As Pink Indigo matures, it develops colonies and spreads by suckering. However, it will not turn into an unmanageable weed, like mint (*Mentha* spp.). The plant is sensitive to cold weather and dies back to the ground in winter. Treat it as you would many perennials and cut it back in early spring. Once it is established, it tolerates dry conditions quite well. It therefore makes an excellent choice for use under large shade trees that compete for water, such as oaks.

Height: 3 feet • Spread: 3–4 feet; makes colonies over time • Moisture: moderately drought-tolerant • Hardiness Zone: 6–8 • Heat Zone: 5–11 (estimated) • Propagation: stem cuttings and dividing clumps

Dwarf Crepe Myrtles

Lagerstroemia hybrids

Most of our information about Crepe Myrtles is presented in the chapter "Large Shrubs and Small/Patio Trees." However, because dwarf Crepe Myrtle varieties are still relatively new, we decided to discuss them separately.

The work done by the late Dr. Don Egolf and his successor Dr. Margaret Pooler at the National Arboretum in Washington, DC, is a priceless gift to the world of horticulture. For more on their work, we again refer you to "Large Shrubs and Small/Patio Trees."

The true dwarf/container varieties of Crepe Myrtle now allow us to grow these wonderful plants anywhere. This is good news for gardeners in USDA Zones 3–5. In the past, these folks have been excluded from the joy of owning a Crepe Myrtle because of too-cold winter temperatures. Now they can enjoy some of these ruffled pink-flowered beauties that others further south sometimes take for granted. Yes, these 2–3 foot plants will have to be kept in containers and lugged indoors for the winter, but at least there is finally an option!

Another plus to dwarf Crepe Myrtles is that two cultivars look terribly similar to Indian Hawthorn (*Raphiolepis indica*). For those of you who live in the higher USDA Zones and have lost your Indian Hawthorns to disease, the 'Pocomoke' and 'Chickasaw' dwarf Crepe Myrtle make excellent replacements. (Our motto: If it croaks, don't plant it again.)

Brian was simply in awe when he first saw 'Pocomoke' and 'Chickasaw' while touring the National Arboretum in Washington, DC. It was late June and Dr. Pooler was showing off some of the Crepe Myrtles currently under evaluation. Brian was impressed that a dwarf *Lagerstroemia* could so closely resemble an Indian Hawthorn. If you can imagine an Indian Hawthorn that blooms in June and July, then that is what 'Pocomoke' and 'Chickasaw' look like.

Height: 2–3 feet • Spread: 1–2 feet • Sun: full sun • Moisture: regular moisture; drought-tolerant when established • Hardiness Zone: 6–9 • Heat Zone: 4–10 • Propagation: easily root as dormant winter cuttings

Small to Medium Shrubs

If you've read the previous chapter on small shrubs, you may still be wondering if there's really an important difference between them and small to medium shrubs. The answer is yes, although it is hard to believe (and even easier to forget) when you see hundreds of attractive, compact, immature woody ornamentals on display at a garden center or nursery. Knowing how big a plant is going to get is a critical step to successful landscaping.

S mall to medium shrubs reach about 3–6 feet at maturity. This size range is quite useful for beds around or in front of a house. However, small to medium shrubs usually make unsuitable foundation plantings and they are certainly not appropriate along walkways that lead to entrances. (Think safety as well as proportion.) They also look silly in front of a bay window that starts 2 ¹/₂ feet from the ground.

Since plants are rarely grown in ideal situations, horticulturists had to allow for variation of size when they created maximum height/width categories. This is because site and soil conditions vary considerably. For example, the environment in your front and back yard is usually never the same. This means that a Butterfly Bush *(Buddleia davidii)* growing on the east side of your property may always be larger than the one planted in a western exposure. Such environmental variables—and there are many—are often beyond our control.

Although small to medium shrubs fit comfortably into diminutive or immense garden sites, they must be appropriately spaced away from structures so as not to interfere with use or upkeep. In spacious settings, these plants are large enough to serve as specimen plants or as mass plantings. However, no matter where or how you decide to use them, remember to allow enough space for their mature height. This might be difficult at the time of planting because youngsters often look so small and insignificant. But three years later, you will definitely be glad that you took the effort to plan for their growth.

Butterfly Bush
Buddleia davidii

Butterfly Bush

Buddleia davidii

Butterfly Bush has become one of the most popular summer-flowering shrubs in America. Dr. Michael Dirr has humorously proclaimed that the gardening public's enthusiasm for this plant has become a mania and a serious disease. He also admits, "To some degree I, too, have been infected." We confess that these plants can indeed be addictive. The allure comes in different forms for different gardeners. The long-panicled, orange-throated flowers that erupt from early June to the last day of fall attract some, while the perpetual fragrance entraps others. Brian loves the intricate detail of each tiny flower, and P.J.

Some Like It Hot Small to Medium Shrubs	
Buddleia davidii	Butterfly Bush
Clethra alnifolia	Clethra, Summer-Sweet
Kerria japonica	Kerria, Japanese Kerria
Mahonia bealei	Leatherleaf Mahonia
M. fortunei	Chinese Mahonia

appreciates the soft silvery green leaves on her lavender specimen plant. And yes, these shrubs attract butterflies—from Monarchs, fritillaries and sulphurs to tiny skippers.

Sticking this plant with a strict botanical definition can be tricky because its temperament changes depending on where it's grown. In many respects, the Butterfly Bush is a perennial. In northern climates it either dies back to the ground or is cut back to 12 inches. So in that respect, it behaves or is treated like most perennials. However, in climates that are more moderate, the Butterfly Bush can become a 5–10 foot woody shrub. It will leaf out from the previous year's wood in the late spring, and if the weather is gentle enough, the Butterfly Bush will keep its leaves throughout the winter.

This shrub has had the attention of plant breeders and selectors for a number of years. So much so, that as many as forty-five varieties of Buddleia are now grown! The result is a wide range of color and leaf texture. Flower colors range from white to lavender to blue to pink to mauve to yellow.

Notwithstanding the danger of catching the Butterfly Bush disease, they're great *Some Like It Hot* plants. These relatively pest-free plants are long-lived and can be cuddled and doted upon or left to fend for themselves. Depending on your climate, you can cut them back each year, or let them develop into a large shrub.

Buddleia is native to the Chinese subtropics. They perform best in full sun although they will tolerate moderate shade. (However, expect flowering to be noticeably reduced.) They need a well-drained soil, so don't try to grow Butterfly Bush in wet areas or where the soil is waterlogged for extended periods. They can achieve a tremendous amount of growth in one growing season, so consider that when choosing your placement in the landscape. Of course, you can always cut it back in the spring if it gets out of hand. Note that we said "spring." Vigorous pruning should be done only when new growth begins. Cutting it back in midsummer will probably not kill the plant, but you will lose any chance of a good flower season. Blooming will remain robust if the plant is occasionally deadheaded throughout the summer.

Height: 5–10 feet • Spread: 4–8 feet • Sun: full sun preferred • Moisture: well-drained soil, but benefits from regular watering • Hardiness Zone: 5–9 • Heat Zone: 3–11 • Propagation: can be rooted from cuttings made in midsummer (June-August) or from winter hardwood. Seeds collected germinate easily, but should be chilled 3–5 weeks before planting. They need light to germinate

Clethra
Clethra alnifolia

Clethra, Summer-Sweet

Clethra alnifolia

We will not bother to describe the horticultural miseries associated with a southern midsummer. Let's just say that finding a shrub that will provide a month's worth of flowering color during our relentless spells of heat and humidity can be difficult. Finding one that also provides fragrance is even tougher. That is why we have come to like Clethra more and more each year.

Clethra is native to the eastern seaboard, the southeast, and eastern Texas. Although it grows naturally in swamps and sandy soils, it is not picky. Its ability to tolerate less than ideal conditions means that it will stand up to the salt of the seashore as well as the burning heat of afternoon sun. Although flower production is best in full sun, Clethra will also bloom in shade. But here is the best part about *C. alnifolia*. In late June or July, just about the time when most of us abandon our gardens until cooler days return, Clethra kicks into a four-week frenzy of efflorescence. The native species yield white flowers while the hybrids exhibit varying shades of pink. Depending on the variety, the panicles are 6–8 inches long. All *C. alnifolias* produce one of the most wonderful continual fragrances you will ever smell.

Clethra's drawbacks are its constant need for water and its tendency to droop. However, its demand for water can be used to your advantage if you have a soggy area. This plant thrives in wet soils, and if you have such a place, Clethra is a perfect choice. But if you intend to grow this plant in a mostly arid location, including dry shade, be forewarned that failure to respect its moisture requirement will lead to disappointment. Once the plant is established, it may be able to withstand less frequent watering, but its overall leaf and bloom vigor will be diminished. The reward for remembering to water regularly is well worth the effort.

Depending on the soil conditions, Clethra's tall, slender stems will reach 6–8 feet in height. This thinness results in drooping branches, although selecting more compact varieties like 'Sixteen Candles' or 'Compacta' will ameliorate the flopping trait. If you insist on owning a well-behaved Clethra, then remember that all varieties tend to grow larger in wet soils than in dry ones. In other words, don't encourage bad behavior.

Clethra's robust rhizome system sprouts suckers that over time will spread into colonies. This means you can divide the clumps like a perennial, thus having a constant supply of plants to use or share. However, you should consider this spreading habit before selecting a spot. While Clethra is the perfect choice for wet areas, it will also perform well in the typical well-drained shrub bed. Even though out-of-bounds colonies are easily dug up and divided, you must allow space for digging. Putting Clethra in a bed where you plan on using flowering bulbs or understory herbaceous materials is not a good idea.

Clethra
Clethra alnifolia

Beginning in the late spring, Clethra puts out dark green foliage with pronounced veination. This late-leafing trait fools many gardeners into thinking it is dead. Don't get caught in this trap. Before pulling all your "dead" Clethra, wait a few more weeks. In the fall, the leaves turn a pale yellow to golden brown, and then drop during the winter.

The varieties available are truly astounding. 'Summer Beauty' is a late-flowering variety that can be used to extend your Clethra growing season. 'Rosea' offers a pink flower that holds its color well in the hot and humid south. From the white flowers of the common 'Hummingbird' to the deep pink flowers of 'Ruby Spice', to the speckled variegation of 'Creel's Calico', you can find a Clethra that is right for you.

Height: 6–8 feet • Spread: 4–6 feet, but spreading wider over time into a colony • Sun: full sun to partial shade • Moisture: likes regular moisture, will do excellently in wet soils • Hardiness Zone: 4–9 • Heat Zone: 3–11 • Propagation: cuttings in midsummer root readily; seeds germinate easily, and large clumps can be divided

Kerria, Japanese Kerria
Kerria japonica

Kerria is a plant most people don't appreciate until it begins to mature. When it is first planted, expect it to look a little sickly. It does not start out as a rapid grower. After a few years, though, the growth rate will increase and the plant will become more appealing. Kerria has an arching kind of growth habit, although the stems grow upright at first. As the plant increases in size, it develops a round, mounded look. This appearance comes from small colonies of suckers. They are similar to the ones seen on Black Chokeberry and Clethra, although they are not quite as vigorous. The spearhead-shaped leaves are 2–4 inches long. This leaf form makes them look longer than they are, which in turn accentuates Kerria's arching growth habit. The stems, which are attractive in their own right, are often bright green in the summer and then turn bright

yellow in the winter. This can add some unusual winter interest to an otherwise drab garden.

Kerria
Kerria japonica

Although Kerria is native to central and western China, it is also found on Japanese mountainsides. For most *Some Like It Hot* gardeners, Kerria is best used as a shade plant, or at least sheltered from the hot afternoon sun. (It's a lot like most southerners; the heat won't bother it as long as it's in the shade.) While it happily grows on sunny moist banks in Japan, our relentless summer sun could lead to root rot problems.

Kerria flowers put on their best show in the middle of spring although the plant will bloom intermittently throughout the rest of the growing season. The bright yellow flowers are quite nice. They are about $1^1/2$ inches across and emerge from the wood of the previous year's growth. This means that if you must prune, it should be done after the first big flowering in the spring. However, do not expect the usual sporadic blooming for the remainder of the season.

The plant's somewhat twiggy spreading growth habit is not well suited for specimen use. Kerria is probably best used in a mass planting where the mounds can grow together and the combined flowers have a synergistic effect. Several varieties exist, including 'Albescens', which offers an off-white flower, and 'Splendens', which sports large, buttercup-shaped flowers.

If you should come across a young planting of Kerria, don't let its scraggly appearance turn you off. Although he has never seen Kerria at full maturity (they've always been about 3 feet tall or less), Brian is convinced that this plant has far more potential than is often believed. While he realizes that not everyone shares these sentiments, he thinks it deserves at least some thoughtful consideration. Its loose growth and long leaves with doubly-serrated leaf margins certainly make it an interesting plant. If an established planting is not accessible to you, then try to find a large containerized plant at a garden center or nursery to base your decision on.

Height: 3–6 feet • Spread: often wider than taller with time • Sun: partial shade to filtered shade • Moisture: well-drained soil, but likes regular watering • Hardiness Zone: 4b–9 • Heat Zone: 1–10 • Propagation: roots easily from soft-wood cuttings in summer and fall. Division of the mound is an easy way to get new plants.

Leatherleaf Mahonia

Mahonia bealei

Some might be surprised that we consider the Leatherleaf Mahonia a *Some Like It Hot* plant. While most folks associate Mahonias with cooler climates, and justifiably so, Leatherleaf Mahonia is a good selection for many of the gardens in hot and humid regions. Both Leatherleaf and Chinese Mahonia (*M. fortunei*) make excellent shade plants in *Some Like It Hot* gardens. While we would never suggest that someone use them in a location where they receive even the tiniest bit of sun, both kinds of plants will add visual interest to a deprived shady spot.

Leatherleaf Mahonia
Mahonia bealei

Leatherleaf Mahonia
   Mahonia bealei

Leatherleaf Mahonia is also an excellent choice for those often-neglected yet always in view shaded tight corner sites. However, we must warn that the spines on Leatherleaf Mahonia can be as brutal as any "sticker bush" in the gardening world. In other words, don't put it at the corner of the walkway where it is likely to be brushed by every passerby. Notwithstanding that one drawback, Leatherleaf Mahonias are attractive plants that can fill many voids in shady areas.

The feature that makes Mahonia a *Some Like It Hot* plant is not the beautiful yellow fragrant flowers, because these flowers appear in late winter or early spring. Their heat-of-summer attractiveness is the fruit. It develops quickly in the spring, and by the onset of hot weather, clusters of grape-like berries appear. As the fruit matures, it takes on a waxy, robin's-egg-blue opaque sheen. Be prepared to share this fabulous display of color with the local wildlife. Evidently, it is a culinary delight.

Leatherleaf Mahonia
Mahonia bealei

Leatherleaf Mahonia is a native of China and enjoys the climates found in the southeast and much of the midwest. While we have never seen a Leatherleaf Mahonia over 5–6 feet tall, they are capable of reaching 12–15 feet in height. Its upright growth habit keeps them from getting very wide. The leaves are pinnately compound, which means that each leaf has many leaflets on a stalk. Each oval leaflet comes equipped with five to seven very prominent—and very lethal looking—stiff spines. However, we still like Leatherleaf Mahonia because of its coarse texture and colorful summer berries. Brian would be disingenuous if he did not admit his attraction to the plant's fragrant flowers. While their time of arrival—early winter and late spring—doesn't exactly fit our *Some Like It Hot* guidelines, we believe their flowers are an added plus.

Height: usually 4–6 feet; can grow to 12–15 feet • Spread: 3–4 feet • Sun: shade • Moisture: regular moisture, but drought-tolerant once established • Hardiness Zone: 7–9 • Heat Zone: 1–10, possibly 11 • Propagation: seeds from fruit

Chinese Mahonia
Mahonia fortunei

Chinese Mahonia is our favorite Mahonia. The foliage is dark green with narrow leaflets, and the spines are not as stiff as the Leatherleaf's. They are therefore relatively harmless. The plant has a more graceful appearance than its *Some Like It Hot* brother. The growth habit is also more rounded than Leatherleaf and the stems are not as stiff. Chinese Mahonia performs better in warm climates than cooler ones, but don't think you can plant it in the sun. The spiked flowers are also yellow but they appear in late summer, which makes this plant a good choice for any shady spot lacking color in late July or August.

As for plant size, it is capable of reaching 5–6 feet high and just as wide. However, most gardeners will only see 4–5 feet high growth with a 2–3 foot spread. We say "most" because nearly all of us kill or rip our plants out of the ground before they reach maturity. This species is one of the Chinese tropical or subtropical Mahonias and therefore will not tolerate cold weather. They will be killed outright when temperatures drop below zero.

Height: 5–6 feet • Spread: 3–4 feet • Sun: shade • Moisture: regular moisture, but drought-tolerant once established • Hardiness Zone: (7) 8–9 • Heat Zone: 7–11 • Propagation: stem cuttings

Chinese Mahonia
Mahonia fortunei

Medium to Large Shrubs

The plants in this chapter are still considered shrubs, but they get a whole lot bigger than most people expect. This is because their mature size is seldom taken into account when they are purchased. Any plant that gets over six feet tall, and sometimes just as wide, is classified as a medium to large shrub.

ike their smaller relatives, their mature size will vary in different site conditions. For example, if an Abelia is planted in its preferred environment, its full-grown height and width should be 5–6 feet tall and 4–5 across. However, if it is put in a less than ideal site, or stuck in poor soil, it will never reach its full growth potential.

Medium to large shrubs will not fit in small landscapes or beds because they are just too big. Instead, they should be seen at a distance along edges and boundaries where they can screen unsightly views and provide privacy. Although any of them could be used as specimen plants, they're also extremely useful in a mixed-shrub border where they add color and interest at different times of the year.

It's unfortunate that most of our larger friends are not often given the space they need. No, these plants don't want wide-open spaces, but they certainly require more than most of us give them. And like the smaller shrubs, when the medium to large ones are given insufficient space, frequent pruning is necessary. This in turn prevents them from attaining their full aesthetic potential.

Edward Goucher Abelia
Abelia ×
'Edward Goucher'

Edward Goucher Abelia

Abelia × 'Edward Goucher'

'Edward Goucher' is a *Some Like It Hot* gardener's good friend. This plant does well in hot and humid places and is relatively pest-free. It performs well year in and year out. The plant will get 3–6 feet tall and just about as wide. It stays in bounds relatively well and needs only occasional pruning to maintain its shape. Hard pruning in late winter will rejuvenate old plants. Its growth habit is round and mounding. The leaves are glossy green, which makes it an attractive shrub when not in flower. The bark along the limbs and twigs exfoliates like crepe myrtles, which gives the plant a unique texture and appealing appearance. The pink flowers are wonderful. It's hard to beat a plant that performs this well, with so little trouble, and continually flowers from early summer until first frost. This is one reason why 'Edward Goucher' has become so popular in landscapes across the U.S. The plant is an excellent performer in USDA Zones 6–9 and in ASHS Heat Zones 3–11. In USDA Zone 5, it will behave like a perennial and die back to the ground each winter. And if winter temperatures are unusually cold, expect it to be killed outright.

The Edward Goucher Abelia can tolerate sun and a little shade. However, count on the flowering to be reduced in shade. It likes well-

Some Like It Hot Medium to Large Shrubs	
Abelia × 'Edward Goucher'	Edward Goucher Abelia
Agarista populifolia	Florida Leucothoe, Tall Leucothoe
Bambusa multiplex	Clump Bamboo
Callicarpa spp.	Beautyberry
C. *acuminata*	Mexican Beautyberry
C. *americana*	American Beautyberry
C. *bodinieri* 'Profusion'	Bodinier Beautyberry
C. *dichotoma*	Purple Beautyberry
Callistemon spp.	Bottlebrush
C. *rigidus*	Stiff Bottlebrush
C. *viminalis*	Weeping Bottlebrush
Calycanthus floridus	Sweet Shrub, Carolina Allspice
Duranta erecta	Golden Dewdrop, Sky Flower
Hydrangea spp.	Hydrangea
H. *macrophylla*	Bigleaf Hydrangea
H. *macrophylla macrophylla*	Mophead Hydrangea
H. *macrophylla normalis*	Lacecap Hydrangea
H. *quercifolia*	Oakleaf Hydrangea
Illicium floridanum	Florida Anise-Tree
I. *parviflorum*	Small Anise-Tree
Indigofera amblyantha	No common name
Loropetalum chinense var. *rubrum*	Pink Flowering Loropetalum, Redleaf Loropetalum

Some Like It Hot Medium to Large Shrubs (continued)

Rhododendron spp.

R. prunifolium	Plumleaf Azalea
R. serrulatum	Hammocksweet Azalea
R. viscosum	Swamp Azalea
Senna corymbosa	Flowery Senna
formerly *Cassia corymbosa*	
S. marilandica	Wild Senna
formerly *Cassia marilandica*	
Stewartia monadelpha	Tall Stewartia
Ternstroemia gymnanthera	Japanese Ternstroemia, Cleyera
Viburnum spp.	
V. awabuki	Awabuki Viburnum
V. macrocephalum	Chinese Snowball Viburnum
V. suspensum	Sandankwa Viburnum
Vitex agnus-castus	Chaste Tree

drained soil and regular moisture although it becomes drought-tolerant once it is established.

The Edward Goucher Abelia is a hybrid of *A. × grandiflora* (Glossy Abelia) and *A. schumannii*. The Glossy Abelia is also a good choice for *Some Like It Hot* gardens. It's almost identical to 'Edward Goucher' except the flowers are white.

Another abelia worth considering is the Chinese Abelia (*A. chinensis*). This plant is one of the parents of the Glossy Abelia, and the grandparent of 'Edward Goucher'. The Chinese Abelia is slightly larger (5–7 feet) and has fragrant white flowers. All three of these abelias are excellent butterfly plants.

Abelias should be planted in areas that receive a good bit of sun. Be cautious about using them too close to the foundation. Most gardeners and, unfortunately, many designers do not allow enough space for abelias' mature size. However, if you are willing to plant them 3–4 feet from the foundation, they will make an attractive accent to any building.

Height: 3–6 feet • Spread: 3–6 feet • Sun: full sun or partial shade • Moisture: regular moisture until established • Hardiness Zone: 6–9 • Heat Zone: 3–11 • Propagation: easily propagated by softwood cuttings. Take cuttings June through August and treat with rooting hormone. Seeds should be sown in flats as soon as ripe

Florida Leucothoe, Tall Leucothoe

Agarista populifolia or *Leucothoe populifolia*

Florida Leucothoe has increased in popularity in recent years and with good reason. This plant is native to the southeast coast, from South Carolina to

Florida, and is usually found along stream banks and in hummocks. This makes it an excellent choice in home gardens where the soil stays too wet or drains poorly. However, it can be used in any location if supplemental watering is provided during extended dry periods.

Florida Leucothoe is a large shrub with a suckering or spreading growth habit. Consequently, it will often develop into multi-stem plants. In most landscapes, the plant will get 8–12 feet tall with arching branches, although it can reach 15 feet or more given the right conditions. The leaves are a glossy dark to light green, and the new foliage has a reddish tint when it emerges in the early spring. Once a healthy plant is established, fragrant white flowers form long racemes in May and last through June.

Florida Leucothoe is a nice, informal plant and its thick growth habit and height make it useful as a natural walkway border. It is also an excellent understory plant around large shade trees. Avoid planting Florida Leucothoe in full sun. It performs best in part to full shade.

Height: 8–12 feet (15+ possible) • Spread: 3–4 feet, but makes colonies over time • Sun: part-day to full-day shade • Moisture: needs regular moisture; likes wet sites • Hardiness Zone: 6–9 • Heat Zone: 5–10 • Propagation: semi-hardwood cuttings in the fall

Clump Bamboo
Bambusa multiplex

Don't mention bamboo to an experienced gardener unless you are certified in CPR. Even whispering the "b" word around someone who has done battle with the stuff can send him or her spinning into a near-coronary event. Saying that bamboo is invasive is an understatement. The stuff is like a stick form of kudzu on steroids. However, some people are so taken with bamboo's lush green qualities that they will plant it anyway, fully expecting to suffer the consequences. We offer a solution. It's one of those few opportunities where one can have it both ways.

Clump Bamboo
Bambusa multiplex

Clump Bamboo
Bambusa multiplex

There are two types of bamboo. The plants to avoid are called "running" bamboos. If you see a plant tag with the words "*Phyllostachys*," "*Pleioblastus*," or "*Sasa*," don't purchase it. (There are other genera, but these three are the most common.) Running bamboos have underground stolons called rhizomes and they spread much the same as Bermuda grass (another heart-stopper for southern gardeners). Running bamboos are just as hard to eradicate as Bermuda grass. Both send out never-ending, incredibly stubborn creeping rhizomes. (Have you ever tried to yank out a handful of Bermuda grass from a flowerbed?) However, better-behaved bamboos with a more genteel habit are available.

Clump bamboo is the bamboo of choice for home landscape situations. It does not spread like the typical bamboo. As the name implies, clump bamboo forms dense clusters of vegetation, much like ornamental grasses and many perennials. Yes, over time clump bamboo will spread, but it will take years to become a nuisance, whereas running bamboo will get out of hand in about three hours.

Clump bamboo will provide the same lush, bushy appeal as the kind we don't like to think about. It makes a terrific screen when several are planted together, or let one go solo as an accent plant. Clump bamboo will grow in full sun or shade, and it is relatively pest-free. In most landscape settings, it will grow 20–40 feet tall. If kept in a container it will often grow about 10–20 feet tall.

Height: 20–40 feet, 10–20 in containers (possible 10–50 feet) • Spread: clump will slowly enlarge as long as the bamboo is alive • Sun: full sun or shade • Moisture: drought-tolerant once established • Hardiness Zone: 8–10 • Heat Zone: 5–11 • Propagation: division of clumps

Beautyberry

Callicarpa spp.

Beautyberry is a group of relatively trouble-free, attractive shrubs that willingly accept our brutal summer climate. When late July and early August roll around in the deep south, the heat and humidity shorten a stroll in the garden to nothing more than a quick spin. However, Beautyberry's colorful display makes that brief venture into the yard worth the effort.

Although over 140 species of Beautyberry exist, several cultivars have become quite popular. They are highly regarded for their drupes, the berry-like fruit clusters that begin to reach maturity in late summer. (Think stone fruit—like a cherry rather than a grape.) While almost all *Callicarpa* perform well in sun or shade, berry production is noticeably better in full sun. If these plants have a drawback, it is the berries' tendency to drop at the slightest touch or strong wind in late autumn. (The exception is *C. bodinieri* 'Profusion'.) If you have never enjoyed a Beautyberry in your landscape, make it a point to add at least a specimen to your garden this year.

American Beautyberry
Callicarpa americana

Mexican Beautyberry

C. acuminata

Mexican Beautyberry is an unknown commodity to most gardeners and many professional horticulturists. As the name implies, this plant is native to Mexico and is at home in hot and humid climates. For those familiar with Purple Beautyberry, the Mexican version looks similar. One difference is that Mexican Beautyberry has dark black berries as opposed to the lavender to purple berries of Purple Beautyberry. The berry clumps on Mexican Beautyberry are very large. This plant does well in full sun and can take western exposures with good results. Mexican Beautyberry is only hardy in USDA Zones 8 and 9, being killed back to the ground each winter. This does not affect the flower or berry production because the plant quickly regrows in the spring and reaches 5–6 feet by the end of summer. Mexican Beautyberry will fit into almost any bed setting. It can be mixed in with small to medium sized perennials and treated as one each spring. Simply remove the dead branches in early spring before new growth begins.

Bob McCartney of Woodlanders Nursery in Aiken, South Carolina, has released a variety called 'Woodlanders'. It is identical to the Mexican species in all respects except that the berries are a raspberry red.

Height: 5–6 feet • Spread: 3–4 feet • Sun: full sun • Moisture: regular moisture • Hardiness Zone: 8–9 • Heat Zone: 7–10 • Propagation: unknown

American Beautyberry
Callicarpa americana

American Beautyberry

C. americana

American Beautyberry is a native North American shrub and well suited for *Some Like It Hot* climates. Commonly found from Maryland to Mexico, this plant performs well in full sun or part shade. Its opposite elliptical leaves are the largest of beautyberries commonly grown. They are pale green, $3^{1}/2$–6 inches long, and have been described by some as "anemic" looking. The plant will get 3–8 feet high in the landscape. The majority of American Beautyberries we have seen are in the 4–6 foot range. The plant's habit is rather loose and open. The small and not very showy flowers appear in early to midsummer on small flower stalks at each leaf axis. If you are not in a hurry, you will notice the light lavender or pink flowers on the plant as you walk by.

The fruit, however, is its main attraction. In midsummer the fruit will begin to ripen and take on the characteristic violet to magenta color it is known for. Because the flowers are on a short stalk at the base of each leaf, the subsequent fruit are arrayed in a tight cluster around the stem of the plant at the leaf base. White-fruited forms are available in which the flowers are white as well.

The best place to use American Beautyberry is in a location where you will get sun for a large part of the day. However, it will also perform well in semi-shade, and produce berries nicely in shade. If you have a shady spot that needs some color, American Beautyberry is a good option to consider.

Height: 3–8 feet • Spread: 3–4 feet • Sun: full sun or partial shade • Moisture: regular moisture until established • Hardiness Zone: 7–11 • Heat Zone: 6–11 • Propagation: softwood cuttings from midsummer through early fall. Seeds can be sown directly after ripening in the fall.

American Beautyberry
Callicarpa americana

Bodinier Beautyberry

C. bodinieri 'Profusion'

The blossoms on the Bodinier, sometimes called 'Profusion', Beautyberry have been described as small and unimportant. Well, maybe. In Zone 8b the flowers appear around the beginning of May and are spent before month's end. However, if you can remember when this shrub blooms, a trip to the garden to admire the delicate lavender flowers growing against the dark green leaves is worth the effort.

Bodinier Beautyberry is a little more compact than its loosely-limbed relatives and is a tad shorter. It grows to about 6–8 feet instead of the usual 8–10 feet. Its upright twiggy appearance is vase-shaped.

The tiny fruits begin to mature in October. The drupes start out looking rather pink, then eventually turn lavender. Even after the leaves have fallen, these will stubbornly cling to the branches. Bodinier Beautyberry's fruit is not considered edible, but it is certainly not poisonous. P.J. got curious about their taste after wondering why the neighborhood birds ignored her plant. The berries didn't taste bad, but they were hardly interesting. She later learned that they're a food of last resort for wildlife. This means that the berries will survive to offer interest to an otherwise drab midwinter garden.

Bodinier Beautyberry is best suited for USDA Zones 6–8. We have been told that it does not like warmer climates. However, P.J. planted hers in mid-August when daytime temperatures were in the nineties and the soil temperature was just as hot. The plant never flinched and not one leaf drooped from transplant shock. 'Profusion' adapts well to either wet or dry situations and, although some berry production might be sacrificed if planted in the shade, it is not a finicky plant.

The Bodinier Beautyberry is named after French missionary Émil Marie Bodinieri (1842–1901) who introduced this plant to Europe. *C. bodinieri* is a native of western and central China, where it was used as a medicinal herb.

Height: 6–8 feet • Spread: up to 8 feet • Sun: full sun to partial shade • Moisture: well-drained • Hardiness Zone: 6–8 • Heat Zone: 3–8 • Propagation: unknown

Purple Beautyberry

C. dichotoma

Purple Beautyberry may be the most popular of beautyberries grown in the U.S. The leaves are significantly smaller than American Beautyberry and the overall growth habit of the plant is tighter. The dark green leaves are 1–3 inches long. The plant will grow 3–6 feet high and spread 4–7 feet wide. The branches tend to arch over and touch the ground as they age. Dr. Michael Dirr calls it "the most graceful and refined of the species." This is high praise from a man noted for his critical eye of plant growth and form.

The plant is native to eastern and central China and Japan. While American Beautyberry does well all the way into Mexico, Purple Beautyberry may have trouble in the hotter AHS Zones of 9–11. The plant can be grown like Butterfly Bush where it is pruned back 2 feet to 18 inches from the ground. However this is not necessary and it can be left as a medium-sized shrub. Prune out dead branches each spring.

Purple Beautyberry
Callicarpa dichotoma

The flowers on Purple Beautyberry appear in midsummer. The pinkish or lavender blossoms are not as easily seen as the American Beautyberry's. If you examine the flower/berry stalk, you will notice that each set arises from the axis of the leaf and stem. It then splits off into two pairs of flower/berry-producing structures. This two-forked flower structure is where the scientific name *dichotoma*, meaning "forked in pairs," comes from.

Purple Beautyberry's lavender to purple fruit appears in mid- to late summer. Unlike many of its cousins, Purple Beautyberry's heavy fruit set is not dependent upon cross-pollination from another species. (Many beautyberries fruit only moderately without another variety/species nearby. Japanese Beautyberry [*C. japonica*] is a recommended pollinator.) So, if you intend to plant a single species of *Callicarpa,* yet expect a robust crop of berries, then we recommend Purple Beautyberry. For more on this topic, read Dr. Dirr's comments on fruit production under "Japanese Beautyberry" in his *Manual of Woody Landscape Plants.*

Purple Beautyberry
Callicarpa dichotoma

Several varieties of Purple Beautyberry exist. A white form called 'Albifructus' is available. However, some white berry forms turn brown much sooner than the typical species. 'Early Amethyst' is a variety that will produce copious amounts of berries and reaches only 3–4 feet tall. 'Issai', which is the Japanese word for "best," is also a nice, compact form of Purple Beautyberry. It, too, gets no taller than about 3–4 feet. Ted Stephens brought 'Spring Gold'—whose new foliage begins as a brilliant gold and turns green as the leaves mature—from Japan to America in late 2000. The berries are purple.

As with American Beautyberry, Purple Beautyberry can be grown in full sun or in shade. If you have the space for planting several kinds of *Callicarpa*, try mixing Purple Beautyberry in with other species to match colors and improve berry production. A well-drained soil is best for Purple Beautyberry, and regular watering will be needed until it is established. Provide supplemental water during extended dry periods.

Height: 3–6 feet • Spread: 4–7 feet • Sun: full sun or shade • Moisture: regular watering until established and supplemental watering in extended dry periods • Hardiness Zone: 5–8 • Heat Zone: 3–9 • Propagation: softwood cuttings from midsummer through early fall. Seeds can be sown directly after ripening in the fall

Bottlebrush

Callistemon spp.

Bottlebrush is the kind of plant that entices gardeners to grow it even if it can't survive the climate. These Australian natives are often limited to the milder regions of the south, and some species will survive only in the almost-frost-free subtropics. The bright red bottlebrush-like flowers appear at the beginning of new growth. Bottlebrush is capable of flowering several times during a growing season, and hummingbirds flock to them. Brian can attest to their irresistibility. He has one planted in a prominent location in his yard and enjoys its flowers and the subsequent hummingbird visits several times a year.

Stiff Bottlebrush

C. rigidus

Stiff Bottlebrush is more cold-hardy than other *Callistemons.* This is why it's probably the most often-planted bottlebrush in the U.S. This erect 10–15 foot plant has a 3–4 foot spread. It produces individual, narrow $1/4$-inch wide lance-like leaves with sharp points. Unlike the Lemon Bottlebrush (*C. citrinus*), which has a pleasing citrus odor when the leaves are crushed, the Stiff Bottlebrush emits a pungent odor when the leaves and stems are crumpled. Notwithstanding small differences, they are very similar in growth and habit, except the Lemon has a more graceful appearance. *C. salignus* is a small tree form with yellow flowers and has a cold-tolerance similar to Lemon Bottlebrush.

Stiff Bottlebrush
Callistemon rigidus

Stiff Bottlebrush is very drought-tolerant and, once it is established, can withstand long periods of dry weather. Brian observed this variety producing flowers four to five times during the drought-plagued growing season of 2002. He then realized what a valuable plant the Stiff Bottlebrush is for water-sensitive gardeners who still want summer-long blooming plants. However, the Stiff Bottlebrush does have its limits. While it is more cold-hardy than its warm-blooded brothers and sisters, it is still a USDA Zone 8–11 plant. Like gardenias, when exposed to direct sunlight on cold, freezing mornings, the trunks of Stiff Bottlebrush will suffer winter injury. The lesson is taken from gardenias: protect the trunks from direct sunlight on freezing mornings.

Fortunately, savvy plantsmen have been working to select Stiff Bottlebrush varieties that are more cold-tolerant. Ted Stephens of Nurseries Caroliniana in North Augusta, South Carolina, has selected a variety called 'Clemson Hardy'. This variety was exposed in winter to -8° F temperatures in Clemson, South Carolina, and experienced no injury. Of course, this extends the possibility of having a bottlebrush in USDA Zone 7 landscapes. 'Woodlanders Hardy' is a variety selected by Bob McCartney of Woodlanders Nursery in Aiken, South Carolina. This plant has also withstood -8° F temperatures.

All bottlebrushes like full sun and well-drained soils. Do not plant them in wet locations or areas where water is held for a long time. Stiff Bottlebrush has moderate salt tolerance for those living near the ocean. However, it should not be exposed to direct salt spray.

Height: 8–15 feet • Spread: 3–4 feet • Sun: full sun • Moisture: drought-tolerant once established • Hardiness Zone: 8–11 • Heat Zone: 7–11 • Propagation: unknown

Weeping Bottlebrush

Callistemon viminalis

Weeping Bottlebrush comes in several sizes. While most cultivars can become small 20–25 foot trees, two compact forms are worth mentioning. 'Captain Cook' reaches 4 feet, as does 'McCaskillii', which has a reputation as a vigorous grower and offers a better flowering selection. Like their larger relatives, these pint-sized versions have branches and flowers that hang straight down like a weeping Mulberry or Cherry tree. No matter what the size, this weeping characteristic makes a positive statement in the landscape.

These plants are only cold-hardy in USDA Zones 9 and higher. However, 'Captain Cook' and 'McCaskillii' should be easy to overwinter in pots if one is willing to put up with the inconvenience of hauling them in and out of doors. The much larger varieties are discussed in "Large Shrubs and Small/Patio Trees."

Height: 4 feet • Spread: 2–3 feet • Sun: full sun • Moisture: regular watering • Hardiness Zone: 9–11 • Heat Zone: 8–12 • Propagation: unknown

Sweet Shrub, Carolina Allspice

Calycanthus floridus

Sweet Shrub is a plant that just made it under the wire as a *Some Like It Hot* plant. The flowers appear in late spring and into early summer. If not for this, we could not have included it in our list. (By some accounts, we should have left it out.) However, its many merits made it a must for inclusion. First, it's a native southeastern plant. Found in moist areas from Virginia to Florida, Sweet Shrub is well suited to the environments of the hot and humid summer. It is also tolerant of all types of soils. The flowers have a fruity fragrance that scents large areas when planted in mass.

Sweet Shrub
Calycanthus floridus

The plant grows to 6–9 feet tall and 6–12 feet wide. The large leaves are dark green with a tough, leather-like appearance. It makes a nice shrub if grown in full sun, but has a reputation as a scraggly little plant when put in shady locations. The flowers are usually a dark wine-red; however, light green and white are now available. For those more interested in fragrance, Dr. Dirr notes that Sweet Shrubs grown from seed are often not fragrant. So, the wise gardener will purchase plants when they are in flower to ensure a fragrant form.

Sweet Shrub performs best in full-sun locations with well-drained, moist soils. If you can accept a less full and more airy plant, Sweet Shrub is an excellent plant for the shade. Most *Some Like It Hot* gardeners will be more pleased with their efforts if the plant is used in a mass planting or as a shrub border. Any way you choose to use it, just enjoy the fragrance of the flowers on an early summer evening as you stroll through the garden. The stems make an excellent cut flower in arrangements, and the fragrant blossoms will scent the room they are in.

Several varieties of Sweet Shrub are in the trade. 'Athens' is a wonderfully fragrant yellow-flowering form. 'Edith Wilder' is a variety of note in the red-flowering types. It can get as tall as 10 feet and is distinguished for its exceptional fragrance. 'Purpureus' is a variety with purplish leaves.

Height: 6–9 feet • Spread: 6–12 feet • Sun: full sun or shade • Moisture: regular moisture • Hardiness Zone: 4–9 • Heat Zone: 3–10 • Propagation: semi-hardwood cuttings taken in midsummer and treated with rooting hormones

Golden Dewdrop, Sky Flower

Duranta erecta

Golden Dewdrop is a little-known plant that has great potential in milder climates of *Some Like It Hot* gardens. It acquires its name from the golden yellow 1/2-inch-diameter berries that form in late summer and hang down in racemes from the branches. One of its other common names is Sky Flower, which comes from the sky-blue flowers that appear in late spring or early summer on new growth. The plant can grow as tall as 18 feet, but it rarely reaches that height in most areas. The plant usually dies back to the ground each winter and then will quickly regrow in the spring. The leaves are a rich green, and in USDA Zones 9 and higher, they are evergreen. Golden Dewdrop likes full sun and a loose, well-drained soil rich in organic matter. The plant can be used as a specimen plant, provided the dieback to the ground can be accepted each winter. For those who don't want a mass of dead wood in a prominent location during the winter, mixing it in with other plant material is a good option.

Height: 4–6 feet (18 feet possible) • Spread: 3–4 feet wide • Sun: full sun • Moisture: regular watering • Hardiness Zone: (7) 8–11 • Heat Zone: 6–11 • Propagation: seeds or cuttings

Hydrangeas

Hydrangeas are becoming more popular than ever. After all, they bloom spectacularly through most of the summer. And what other plant lets the gardener control the flowers' fabulous range of colors and hues? It's no wonder that practically every gardener wants to own at least one traditional Mophead.

Hydrangeas have reached the point where they are almost an entity unto themselves—much like azaleas and camellias. Like the azalea or camellia specialist, it is now possible to devote an entire horticultural career to hydrangeas. An exciting recent breakthrough is varieties that will rebloom. One named 'Endless Summer' is now available at garden centers. As more repeat-bloomers make it to the marketplace, they will certainly accelerate the hydrangeas' popularity. We will focus on three of the most sought-after hydrangea cultivars—Mopheads, Lacecaps, and Oakleaf Hydrangeas.

Bigleaf Hydrangea

Hydrangea macrophylla

Bigleaf Hydrangeas are divided into two groups, Mopheads (or Hortensia), and Lacecaps. The difference is in the flower. Mopheads, as the name implies, have large florets that appear in a rounded ball like a mop head. Lacecaps have florets arranged in a pinwheel fashion. The showy sepals are on the outer portion of the flower and the non-showy fertile florets are on the inner portion. While Mopheads and Lacecaps are sufficient terms to differentiate the two for us, in botanical circles the use of such easy terms is heresy. When you are looking at the botanical names of Mophead and Lacecap Hydrangeas, look for the additional identifier of their subspecies, often abbreviated "subsp." For Mopheads, the identifier is "subsp. *macrophylla*," although sometimes it will be listed as just "*macrophylla*." For Lacecaps, the identifier is "*normalis*." Looking at the tag of a Mophead Hydrangea, the botanical name should read "*Hydrangea macrophylla* subsp. *macrophylla*" or "*H. macrophylla mac.*" For the Lacecap Hydrangea, the botanical name should read "*Hydrangea macrophylla* subsp. *normalis*" or "*H. macrophylla normalis*."

Mophead Hydrangea
Hydrangea macrophylla
macrophylla

Lacecap Hydrangea
Hydrangea macrophylla normalis

Outside of the flower differences, which are significant, these two types of Bigleaf Hydrangea share the same aspects. They both require afternoon shade and should avoid full sun in USDA Zones 7–9. They both need to be planted in a well-drained, rich soil and will need frequent watering. Bigleaf Hydrangeas also have a high salt tolerance that makes them a useful seashore plant. Although the plant can withstand some direct salt spray, placing it on the windward side of the beachfront may be hazardous to its overall well-being. Instead, use it on the leeward side of the beachfront block, away from the ocean.

One important aspect in the care of Mopheads and Lacecaps is pruning. For most deep south gardeners, Lacecaps and Mopheads bloom in midsummer, during June and July. As many have discovered, pruning Mophead Hydrangeas is often an act of frustration. This is because the plant produces flowers on the previous season's growth. Therefore, if you prune it in the spring or late winter, you will lose its flowers. Because the flowers are set in the late summer for the next year's bloom season, the only time to prune is in the middle of summer. However, that is often when the inflorescence is still abundant, so pruning will remove the flowers you have been waiting all summer to enjoy. It is a Hobson's choice. The best advice is to prune before August 1st and not at all after that date. Fortunately, repeat-bloomers flower off of new growth. This should give *Some Like It Hot* gardeners the chance to prune in early spring and still get flowers in the summer. Lacecap Hydrangeas are more forgiving on the pruning front. They can be pruned immediately after flowering and still provide flowers the next summer.

Most Mophead Hydrangea flower colors can be influenced by soil pH. A lower pH of 5.0–5.5 will produce blue flowers, while a higher pH of 6.0–6.5 will often produce pink ones. Brian came up with a mnemonic device to help him remember how to change the colors: "You have to get low to get the blues."

The best place to use Bigleaf Hydrangeas in most *Some Like It Hot* gardens is in a location that gets morning sun and afternoon shade. We have seen them flower nicely in areas where they receive filtered sunlight most of the day and only an hour or two of direct sun. However, don't offer Bigleaf Hydrangeas too much shade, or you may not get any flowers. Place these plants in a well-drained, rich soil and expect to water them regularly. Do not place them in hot, dry areas of your landscape because the results will be disappointing.

There are over five hundred varieties of Bigleaf Hydrangeas. We could never discuss them all, but here are a few noteworthy mentions. In the Mophead types, 'Dooley' is renowned for its cold-hardiness. It can withstand cold temperatures, which means that it won't suffer from damaged wood or flower buds. Some growers report getting reblooming on Dooley. (For those who like plant trivia, 'Dooley' is named after the famous University of Georgia Football coach Vince Dooley, who has become an accomplished horticulturist since his retirement from college football.) 'Forever Pink' is a notable variety because it is a Mophead that blooms on new growth. The new variety called 'Endless Summer' is also a repeat-bloomer that flowers on each flush of new growth. 'Nigra', sometimes-called 'Black Stem', is a variety with black to dark purple stems. A new release from Ted Stephens of Nurseries Carolina named 'Fuji Waterfall' is a white double-flowering form with flowerheads 12 inches across. They cascade down from the flowerhead and will repeat flowering clear into the fall.

When considering a Lacecap Hydrangea, 'Kardinal Red' is a nice variety that provides red flowers. 'Geoffrey Chadbud' will produce pink flowers and 'Larnarth White' will have white ones.

Height: 4–6 feet • Spread: 3–4 feet • Sun: afternoon shade to all-day filtered sunlight • Moisture: water regularly • Hardiness Zone: 6–9 • Heat Zone: 5–10 • Propagation: softwood cuttings taken May–July; air layering. Many hydrangeas will readily produce offspring under the plant from seeds. However, the seeds are dust-like and difficult to handle

Oakleaf Hydrangea
Hydrangea quercifolia

Oakleaf Hydrangea

H. quercifolia

Oakleaf Hydrangea is a woefully underused shade-tolerant yet summer-flowering shrub. However, before the arrival of 'Pee Wee' and other dwarfing types, it is easy to understand why they were ignored. Oakleaf Hydrangeas can reach sizes of 8–12 feet, although they will most often stay in the 4–6 foot range. Their growth habit is upright with sparse branching. The large oak-shaped leaves are deep green and are 3–8 inches long, and as wide. The leaf size gives the plant a very coarse texture, which, from a design perspective, makes incorporating this hydrangea into the landscape difficult. However, if you have a shady area where you want color, then this is a good choice.

Oakleaf Hydrangeas produce white flower spikes as long as 12 inches and 3–4 inches wide. Their large size will often weigh a branch over. The flowers appear white in early summer. As the summer progresses, they will change to purplish pink, and finally to tan. The dried flower heads remain into fall, which offers additional interest. Any gardener would be grateful for such an extended and varied color display. However, the Oakleaf Hydrangea has even more to offer. As the cool nights of fall establish themselves, the leaves on some varieties turn to red, orange, or purple.

Another aesthetically appealing feature of the Oakleaf Hydrangea is its bark. Often unnoticed because of the large leaves and flowers, the bark will exfoliate like a Crepe Myrtle, leaving a cinnamon-brown stem color. The plants tend to sucker and develop spreading colonies over time. However, with the attention this plant will attract in your garden, colonies simply provide an easy method for sharing it with friends.

Oakleaf Hydrangeas
Hydrangea quercifolia

We have seen Oakleaf Hydrangeas in various settings. In cooler climes, they can be used in full sun. However, in the warmer climates of AHS Zones 7–10, they will definitely need some shade. Mulching around the roots or planting them in a site that offers a cool, moist root zone will produce the best results. While the plant is not a water hog, it does need regular watering in a well-drained soil. Once the plant is established, it is, for the most part, pest- and maintenance-free.

If you are going to plant an Oakleaf Hydrangea, it is best to locate your plant where it will receive filtered sun all day long, or even some afternoon shade. The plant will perform wonderfully under a canopy of large trees. It also appreciates the eastern side of a building, and possibly the north side as well. Just as in real estate, the three most important factors in gardening are "location, location, and location." If you want a robust Oakleaf Hydrangea, give it cool, moist roots. Put down 2–3 inches of good organic mulch around the root area. (Rock mulches do not meet this criterion.) At the risk of boring longtime southern gardeners, we emphasize the difference between a moist root zone

Pee Wee
Oakleaf Hydrangea
Hydrangea quercifolia
'Pee Wee'

and wet soil. Oakleaf Hydrangea will not perform well in wet sites.

Thanks to plant breeders, Oakleaf Hydrangea cultivars have become more useful to home gardeners over the past decade. 'Alice' is a variety that was discovered by Dr. Dirr on the University of Georgia campus. She can achieve heights of 12 feet, and the flowers, which turn from white to pink, will be 8–14 inches long. The leaves change to a burgundy red in the fall. 'Alison', another variety discovered by Dr. Dirr on the UGA campus, has flower and leaf color similar to 'Alice'. The flowers are not as large (only 8–10 inches long), and are held more upright on the plant. 'Pee Wee' is one of the more exciting introductions of the past several years. Brian is impressed with its compact form that keeps the plant from growing more than 3–4 feet tall. The smaller size makes it more practical for many gardens than the typical species. 'Pee Wee' has 4–5 inch white flowers. The fall leaf color climaxes to a rose, then turns reddish-purple. Brian has this variety in his garden and is most impressed by its resilience, flower color, form, and fall leaf color. 'Snow Queen' is an older variety that has 6–8 inch flowers turning from white to pink, with reddish-bronze fall leaf color. 'Snowflake' has double flowers 12–15 inches long, with maroon fall color.

Height: 4–6 feet (10–12 possible) • Spread: 3–6 feet • Sun: afternoon shade to all-day filtered sunlight • Moisture: water regularly • Hardiness Zone: 5–9 • Heat Zone: 5–10 • Propagation: softwood cuttings taken May–July; air layering. Many hydrangeas will readily produce offspring under the plant from seeds. The seeds are dust-like and difficult to handle

Florida Anise-Tree
Illicium floridanum

Florida Anise-Tree is native to the southeast and is found in wet areas in parts of Florida, Alabama, Mississippi, and Louisiana. *Illicium floridanum* also occurs in Georgia, but in only one county. Discovered there in 1980, state officials are now determined to keep its habitat from literally drying up. Drained wetlands and diverted streams are Florida Anise-Tree's biggest enemy.

Because hot and humid conditions suit it, many southern gardeners use this dependable broadleaf evergreen as an anchor for their landscape. Although this plant has excellent cold tolerance and rarely has pest problems, it will rebel against full sun exposure. If given too much sun during our hot summers, Florida Anise-Tree will sulk by turning its leaves light green. Expect growth to be a little sluggish if it is not planted in shade. When planted in the correct spot, the leaves are a wonderful dark green.

Each leaf is 2–6 inches long and about 1–3 inches wide. Its overall appearance reminds many of mountain laurel (*Kalmia latifolia*). However, three identifying characteristics distinguish the Florida Anise-Tree: First, the leafstalks (petioles) are reddish, which also adds interest to the plant. Second, when the leaves are crushed, they emit a spicy odor that is reminiscent of anise. This trait may be the reason insects do not feed on this plant. It is also probably why deer place it at the bottom of their home-landscape preference list.

The third identifying characteristic is the flower. Deep maroon strap-like petals radiate from the center, making it resemble a small, tentacled sea creature. This analogy is quite appropriate because the flower does indeed smell like fish. Fortunately, this odor is not as powerful as real fish, so, unless you plan to make a bouquet, the peculiar smell will not hinder your enjoyment of the Florida Anise-Tree.

The 1–2 inch wide flowers appear in late spring / early summer, and the light brown, star-shaped seedpods develop from August to October. *Some Like It Hot* gardeners now have a choice of maroon, pink, or white flowers as well

Florida Anise-Tree
Illicium floridanum

True Pink
Florida Anise-Tree
Illicium floridanum
'True Pink'

as variegated foliage. 'Halley's Comet' (sometimes spelled Haley) is probably the variety of choice if you prefer maroon. It has the added benefit of a longer bloom period than most other types. For the white flower form, 'Semmes' is probably the best choice because it has a heavier bloom set and is more restrained in its growth rate.

This plant, like most swamp plants, tends to form suckering colonies. Although Florida Anise-Tree is not as vigorous as others, it will eventually form a small 6–10 foot spreading mound. While its growth habit is slightly open and airy, it can be made more compact with a little tip-pruning while it is still young.

Florida Anise-Tree is a good plant to use where you need a relatively large shrub in a somewhat difficult situation. It will do well in a dry or wet shady spot and will tolerate full sun with wet or dry soil if you are willing to accept light green leaves. This plant was truly made for a *Some Like It Hot* garden. Its ability to thrive in hot and humid conditions makes it worthy of being in the garden for this trait alone.

Height: 6–10 feet • Spread: 5–15 feet • Sun: best in half-day shade to shade; will grudgingly take full sun • Moisture: tolerates wet or dry conditions • Hardiness Zone: 6–9 • Heat Zone: 5–10 (11) • Propagation: semi-hardwood and hardwood cuttings taken in late summer and winter. Also root cuttings from suckering plants

Small Anise-Tree
Illicium parviflorum
Small Anise-Tree has all the features *Some Like It Hot* gardeners expect, except for one—showy flowers. Despite the fact that the blossoms are pretty, they go virtually unnoticed unless you know it's time to expect them. They appear in early summer around May and last into June. Notwithstanding this uneventful occurrence, Small Anise-Tree is still a great plant because it tolerates all

kinds of growing conditions. It is native to the southeast and is found throughout wet areas of Florida and Georgia. This, of course, makes it well suited to hot and humid conditions.

The leaf colors emerge as a light green at the beginning of the year and then darken to olive green. The leaves grow at a 45-degree angle from the stem, which gives the plant a unique appearance. Like its cousin, *I. floridanum*, Small Anise-Tree leaves smell like anise when crushed. But this plant throws in the additional kick of licorice. Small Anise-Tree will grow to 8–10 feet tall, but can reach 20 feet. Its growth habit is upright, but the plant tends to sucker and produce colonies over time.

Small Anise-Tree is a good plant to use if you need a relatively large shrub in a somewhat difficult situation. It will do well in a dry or wet shady spot and will perform equally well in full sun with or without dry soil.

Height: 8–10 feet (15–20 feet possible) • Spread: 3–5 feet • Sun: full sun or shade • Moisture: tolerates wet or dry conditions • Hardiness Zone: 6–9 • Heat Zone: 5–10 (11) • Propagation: semi-hardwood and hardwood cuttings taken in late summer and winter. Also root cuttings from suckering plants

Small Anise-Tree
Illicium parviflorum

Indigofera amblyantha

This indigo, which has no common name, is one of the more exciting plants for *Some Like It Hot* gardens. It really is one of those "must have" plants because it will fit into anyone's landscape situation as long as it's given full sun. *I. amblyantha* likes heat so much that it seems to devour full sun like candy.

The plant grows 4–6 feet tall during the growing season and could be left that size throughout the winter. However, like all indigos, it flowers on new growth, so giving it a severe pruning in the early spring is time well spent. The 3–5 inch flower stalks appear in late spring and last until the first frost. A newly planted shrub will produce flowers in only a few short weeks and, by midsummer, a 4–6 foot plant will be covered in rich pink flowers that will make even the most macho man admit that pink is pretty. The flower stalks are held upright on the branch. The leaves are compound with seven to eleven $1/2$- to 1-inch oval grayish-green leaflets.

The only reason *I. amblyantha* is not currently being clamored for and devoured by the gardening public is lack of awareness. This is unfortunate, because Brian has seen gardeners go to great lengths to obtain this plant after they see it or hear about it. It doesn't even matter if the plant is not blooming—they will still move heaven and earth to own one.

The physical beauty of this indigo is matched by its affinity for hot and humid conditions. It's as if its performance gets better as the summer heat increases. It is also easily adapted to various soil pHs. While no literature discusses its salt tolerance, we suspect that it would also make an excellent seashore plant, perhaps not along the beach, but where saline conditions are present.

I. amblyantha can be used as large herbaceous perennial or as part of a border planting. Just remember to cut it back each spring. The only thing a gardener needs to take into consideration is the need for full sun. Based on the information we've found, it appears that planting this indigo in shade will lead to disappointing results. But since almost everyone has a spot in their landscape that faces the brutally hot western exposure, finding a place for this plant should not be a problem. *I. amblyantha* is native to China.

Height: 4–6 feet (can be taller if left unpruned) • Spread: 3–4 feet • Sun: full sun • Moisture: regular watering • Hardiness Zone: 6–8 • Heat Zone: 5–9 (10) • Propagation: hardwood cuttings taken in December. Seeds soaked in hot water (190° F) or for 24 hours

Pink Flowering Loropetalum, Redleaf Loropetalum

Loropetalum chinense var. *rubrum*

Pink Flowering Loropetalums have become the rage in southern gardens. Some have even declared these shrubs as one of the most significant plant introductions of the nineties. If one gets the privilege to watch these plants up close for a whole season, their popularity becomes obvious. The foliage emerges with

hues of red to burgundy; then, depending on the variety, the leaves eventual-ly change to a dark green. Pink flowers appear in late spring then continue spo-radically throughout the rest of the growing season. Loropetalum gets its name from the flower shape. *Loro* is Latin for "strap" and describes a narrow leather strap on a shoe. *Petalum* refers to the petals on the flower. So, "Loropetalum" means "flower with narrow strap-like petals." The plant's abundance of flow-ers is simply captivating. Depending on the variety, this shrub typically grows 4–15 feet high. Some plants are currently being grown into breathtaking multi-trunk tree forms.

Redleaf Loropetalum
Loropetalum chinense
var. *rubrum*

Redleaf Loropetalum
Loropetalum chinense
var. *rubrum*
'Zhuzhou Fuchsia'

The Pink Flowering Loropetalum is native to the Hunan, Jiangxi, and Zhejiang provinces of China. (An American geographical analogy would include an area from South Carolina to Florida and over to east Texas.) These provinces are on the southeastern coast of China where the annual precipitation ranges from 40 to 70 inches per year. The city of Shanghai sits at the northern tip of the Zhejiang province. When you consider that Shanghai (31.14 N) and Charleston, South Carolina (32.46 N) share almost identical northern geographical positions, you begin to see why these Loropetalums do so well in our climate. Their USDA Zones range from 7 to 11.

The only thing more rapid than this plant's rise to popularity is the speed at which new varieties are being introduced. Some cultivars to look for when you are Loropetalum hunting are 'Ruby', which is a smaller form that only gets 4–6 feet tall, and 'Suzanne', another small form. 'Burgundy' will grow 6–10 feet tall and is more upright in its growth habit. Ever since Pink Flowering Loropetalums were introduced, 'Burgundy' and another variety named 'Blush' have been the industry's standard. However, 'Blush' is tighter in its growth habit and reaches 8 feet tall and as wide. 'Blush', Razzleberri™, 'Piroche', and 'Daybreak's Flame' are all the same plant with different market names. 'Bicolor' is a form with maroon foliage and white flowers with tinges of pink in the petals. 'Zhuzhou Fuchsia' was introduced to the State Botanical Garden of Georgia in Athens in 1991. It had been growing in the city of Zhuzhou, China, as an ornamental for many years. Known for its almost black maroon leaf, this variety has better cold tolerance than most Loropetalums. It will reach heights of 8–10 feet, perhaps more. Some growers are training this variety into a tree form. Ask for it if you have the space for a small tree.

Height: 4–15 feet • Spread: 4–8 feet • Sun: full sun or partial shade • Moisture: regular watering • Hardiness Zone: 7–9 • Heat Zone: 6–10 • Propagation: stem cuttings taken in the summer

Azaleas

Rhododendron spp.

If you have never heard of summer-blooming azaleas, then the idea of including rhododendrons in a book about hot and humid summer gardening may seem a little crazy. And if you are one of those unfortunate souls who has helplessly watched a *phomopsis*- or *phtyophora*-infested Southern Indica or Kurume melt away in the heat of summer, then this idea seems truly insane. However, we are referring to our very own southeastern *native* azaleas. These indigenous shrubs grow in wet thickets near the edge of the forest. They readily accept our region's heat, humidity, and less than perfect soil conditions.

The native Swamp, Hammocksweet, and Plumleaf Azaleas bloom much later than their imported evergreen cousins. By adding them to your collection, it is possible to have continual azalea bloom for approximately five months. However, we offer a caveat about the bloom periods. We have included only the times for the central portion of the southeast. For a more accurate schedule in your location, we recommend the late Fred Galle's definitive work titled *Azaleas.* He lists a bloom chart with adjustment dates for various locations around the world.

Swamp Azalea
Rhododendron viscosum

Although Swamp, Hammocksweet, and Plumleaf Azaleas can tolerate full sun if well cared for, they will perform their best if afforded afternoon shade. We cannot stress this enough. Although sun is needed for flower production, one must not forget that, in order for them to thrive in captivity, we must make them feel at home. While the Swamp and Hammocksweet Azalea are fond of wet sites, you can successfully grow them in any spot of your garden. Just keep in mind that you will have to experiment with the soil and sun exposure to find the right amount of moisture for them. The Plumleaf Azalea is less demanding of water than the Swamp or Hammocksweet, but you give up the fragrant flowers.

Because these three plants have never been bred or selected for compact growth, they have kept their natural open and wispy growth habit. This means that you should expect to see a lot of trunk and limbs through the foliage. It won't be like looking solely at bark and twigs, but don't anticipate the full look of hollies or evergreen azaleas either. Needless to say, their open growth habit doesn't help them as specimen plants. A single one in a bed may be a little disappointing, especially when it's not blooming. (The exception would be using one to shape into a small tree form.) We recommend using them in a mass, with at least three or five shrubs planted together.

Most everyone thinks of azaleas as evergreen. That's one of the reasons why Southern Indica and Japanese (Kurume) azaleas are so popular. On the other hand, our native azaleas, whether they're spring or summer bloomers, are deciduous. This, of course, means that they will lose their leaves in the winter. We suspect this is why our native azaleas have been relegated to near obscurity in the home landscape. We hope that *Some Like It Hot* gardeners will discover their value; we long to see them take their deserved place in America's home gardens.

Plumleaf Azalea

R. prunifolium

The Plumleaf Azalea has orange-red to red flowers that appear in mid-June and last through the rest of the summer—perhaps into September. This may be a somewhat regional phenomenon, so not all *Some Like It Hot* gardens may get blooms that late. Unfortunately, the flowers are not fragrant, but its late flowering time and extended blooming period make this azalea worth its weight in gold. The plant will grow to 8–10 feet tall. It should be used in partial shade to protect the flowers from the heat of the summer sun. The plant is native to southwestern Georgia and eastern Alabama. Galle states in his book that the first plant was discovered in Cuthbert, Georgia in 1913. It does well in USDA Zones 7–9 and in AHS Heat Zones 4–11. It can be propagated easily from softwood cuttings. Although several varieties of this azalea are known, few are found in the trade. A few varieties of note are 'Coral Glow', which has pink-orange blossoms, 'Peach Glow' with orange-pink flowers, and 'Lewis Shortt', which sends out scarlet red flowers.

Height: 8–10 feet • Spread: 3–4 feet • Sun: partial shade is best, to shade • Moisture: regular moisture, but drought-tolerant once established • Hardiness Zone: 7–9 • Heat Zone: 4–11 • Propagation: softwood cuttings

Hammocksweet Azalea

R. serrulatum

The Hammocksweet Azalea begins blooming at the end of June and continues into August. The flowers are very fragrant, which makes summer mornings a pleasant time to walk through the garden. Its fragrance has been described as clove-like. Flower color ranges from pink to white. This azalea can grow as tall as 15 feet, which affords the opportunity of turning it into a tree. While the Hammocksweet and the Swamp Azalea are often confused, a major difference between the two is that the Hammocksweet is not stoloniferous. The Hammocksweet Azalea is native to the coastal plains of Georgia, Florida, and the Gulf Coast to Louisiana, and is hardy in USDA Zones 7–10 and in AHS Heat Zones 4–11.

Height: 10–15 feet • Spread: 3–4 feet • Sun: partial shade to shade • Moisture: very tolerant of wet sites, but will do well in any soil with regular watering. • Hardiness Zone: 7–10 • Heat Zone: 4–11 • Propagation: softwood cuttings

Swamp Azalea

R. viscosum

The Swamp Azalea begins flowering in May and continues for about a month. The plant has an open, wispy habit, so you must be willing to live with a less-than-dense shrub. The straight species flowers are white, emit a spicy fragrance, and have a shape similar to other native azaleas. This azalea was the first North American one grown in England. It also became the parent of many of the

Swamp Azalea
Rhododendron viscosum

early hybrid deciduous azaleas. The plant is native from Florida to Maine, across through Ohio, and as far west as Texas. It is found along marshy areas and stream banks. The plant's growth habit is stoloniferous, so it spreads by suckers and clumps like Clethra. (This is a common trait among swamp plants.) The height is variable from low-growing 3 feet to as tall as 15 feet. In most landscapes, it should be expected to reach the 8–10 foot range. Cuttings or clump division easily propagate the plant. The plant is hardy in USDA Zones 4–9 and in AHS Heat Zones 4–11.

Several Swamp Azalea varieties have been developed. 'Arpege' is a warm yellow form, 'Pink Rocket' has small pink flowers, and 'Soir de Paris' has dark pink flowers with orange blotches. 'Jolie Madame' is a pink-flowering form with golden blotches.

Height: 3–15 feet, 8–10 feet most often • Spread: 3–10 feet in clumps • Sun: partial shade to shade • Moisture: very tolerant of wet sites, but will do well in any soil with regular watering • Hardiness Zone: 4–9 • Heat Zone: 4–11 • Propagation: stem cuttings or division of clumps

Senna

Cassia spp. is now classified as *Senna* spp.

Sennas (Cassias) are a group of plants on the rise in professional horticulture circles. This assembly of plants is still not quite understood, as a lot of the information about them remains sketchy. Of course, these factors greatly inhibit their use in the home garden. Cassias, as of this writing, are still short on horticultural literature that can aid the professional or novice gardener in understanding and identifying them.

Many of the plants in this group are very similar in appearance. Flowery Senna's appearance is very similar to that of Wild Senna, which causes plenty of trouble for the horticulturist trying to determine which species he's looking at. The Achilles' heel of Cassias is their cold hardiness. Many are USDA Zone 9 or higher plants. Educate yourself on which species will successfully grow in your zone before going to the garden center. Our advice is to take your time in selecting this plant and try to work with a professional who can help you get the plant you need.

Flowery Senna

Senna corymbosa, formerly *Cassia corymbosa*

Flowery Senna will be well received by those *Some Like It Hot* gardeners who can get it to overwinter in their landscapes. If you live in USDA Zones 8–11, this beautiful evergreen (or semi-evergreen) cassia can be successfully grown throughout the year. The dark green leaves have a nice, diamond/lance shape and the rich color holds through winter. If you are willing to put up with a shrub that dies back to the ground each winter, then gardeners in colder climates can at least appreciate it during warmer months. This plant is capable of reaching 10 feet in height and, if winter injury is absent, will spread 4–5 feet wide. The habit is rounded, as the branches tend to spread out instead of up as many other of the Cassias do. Starting at about the end of July, Flowery Senna will begin to produce flat-topped flower clusters, or corymbs, of bright yellow broad flowers. The petals open almost to a full 90 degrees from the flower stalk and create a flower that is almost 2 inches from tip to tip. The plant will be covered in these yellow flowers from the time they start blooming in late summer until the first frost. Flowery Senna adds a delightful bright color to the landscape at a time of year when almost every other plant has retreated from the summer heat.

Flowery Senna is native to Argentina and performs well in the milder climates of USDA Zones 8–11. In Zones 7 and lower, it will experience significant winter injury or outright death. Flowery Senna does well in full sun or half-day shade. It needs a well-drained rich soil with regular moisture. Use it as a specimen or in mass plantings.

Flowery Senna
Senna corymbosa

Flowery Senna
Senna corymbosa

Because the bright yellow flowers appear at a time when little else is blooming, it lends itself as specimen plant or at least deserves a prominent location in the landscape to add color at that otherwise dull time of year.

Height: 6–10 feet • Spread: 4–5 feet • Sun: full sun or half-day shade • Moisture: regular watering • Hardiness Zone: 8–11 • Heat Zone: 7–11 • Propagation: seeds or cuttings taken in March

Wild Senna

Senna marilandica, formerly *Cassia marilandica*

Wild Senna is a North American native Cassia that is better suited for gardeners in Zones 7. Wild Senna will produce the same yellow flowers in late summer as Flowery Senna, but it is not an evergreen plant. Wild Senna will die back to the ground in the winter in USDA Zones 7–10, and may be root-hardy in Zone 6 as well. However, it quickly regrows each spring and early summer and produces a flowering shrub by late summer. Its appearance is almost identical to Flowery Senna. It will grow 4–6 feet tall with a bushy and rounded growth habit of 4–6 feet wide. It, too, prefers full sun, but performs well in half-day shade.

Height: 4–6 feet • Spread: 4–6 feet • Sun: full sun or half-day shade • Moisture: regular watering • Hardiness Zone: 7–10 • Heat Zone: 6–11 • Propagation: seeds or cuttings taken in March

Tall Stewartia

Stewartia monadelpha

Most Stewartias are very intolerant of hot conditions. Therefore, native deep south gardeners may know nothing about them. However, for those transplants from cooler haunts, Stewartias are well known and loved. Wouldn't it be nice to see an old familiar friend in your southern landscape? Tall Stewartia is the only viable choice for *Some Like It Hot* gardeners in AHS Zones 7–9. It has consistently shown better heat tolerance than any other Stewartia. The only challenge is its size.

If you want Tall Stewartia in your landscape, you need space, because the plant can get 20–30 feet tall with a spread of 15–25 feet. In its native habitat of Japan, the tree reaches 80 feet tall! Fortunately, Tall Stewartia almost never attains that height in the U.S.

Tall Stewartia has a shrubby, often multi-trunk growth habit. The leaves are of medium size, reaching 2–3 inches long and 1 inch wide. The leaves hold through the first part of winter, and Tall Stewartia may be become an ever-green plant in USDA Zones 8 and 9. The leaves in most USDA Zones will change to a reddish or maroon color in the fall. Even in USDA Zone 8, this plant offers the possibility of fall leaf color.

The flowers are small and can be difficult to see through the thick foliage. They emerge in midsummer and will continue blooming for about a month. The individual blooms are 1–1^{1}/2 inches across with five white petals that remain in a cup shape. This characteristic prohibits the flowers from opening as wide as other Stewartia flowers. It also helps to hide them among the summer foliage. However, careful examination of the flower will reveal yellowish stamens set among white petals. This attractive appearance is reminiscent of camellia flowers. In fact, most Stewartia flowers have this attribute, and the scientific name for Japanese Stewartia is *S. pseudocamellia*.

Tall Stewartia also has attractive bark. It becomes scaly and exfoliates much like a River Birch (*Betula nigra*), although not as profusely. As the plant matures, the bark takes on a cinnamon color and becomes smoother, often resembling a Crepe Myrtle.

If you decide to use Tall Stewartia in a *Some Like It Hot* garden, it should be used in a shaded area. Choose a location with morning sun and afternoon shade or all-day filtered shade. The soil must be well-drained and contain plenty of good organic matter. As with any plant, a thorough mulching around the roots will make a big difference and, in some situations, *all* the difference. While Tall Stewartia will benefit from regular watering, it is very tolerant of dry soils once it is established. Tall Stewartia's cultural requirements

Japanese Ternstroemia
*Ternstroemia
gymnanthera*

make it an excellent understory tree around large shade trees.

Height: 20–30 feet • Spread: 15–25 feet • Sun: half-day shade or all-day filtered sun • Moisture: drought-tolerant once established • Hardiness Zone: 6–8 • Heat Zone: 5–9 • Propagation: semi-hardwood cuttings taken in midsummer and treated with a rooting hormone; air layering

Japanese Ternstroemia, Cleyera

Ternstroemia gymnanthera

Japanese Ternstroemia was first known in the U.S. as *Cleyera japonica*. However, after several years of commercial cultivation, it was discovered the plant had been misidentified when it was first brought to America from Japan. Japanese Ternstroemia was then correctly renamed *Ternstroemia gymnanthera*. The plant is native to a slew of climatic regions that are accustomed to heat and humidity—Japan, China, Borneo, India, and Korea. This explains why it does so well in the steamy south. It is also relatively pest- and maintenance-free. With the loss of Redtips (*Photinia × fraseri*) in many areas because of *Entomosporum* leaf spot, Japanese Ternstroemia is a popular alternative for a replacement.

Japanese Ternstroemia's new leaves begin red and turn glossy green as they age. The plant's growth habit is upright, so it makes an excellent hedge. Although it can grow as tall as 20 feet, it is easily maintained at any desired height with yearly pruning. The flowers appear in midsummer as small white blossoms on wood from the previous year's growth. Because the plant is often pruned back in the early spring to maintain a hedge appearance, few people ever see the flowers.

Japanese Ternstroemia is a nice plant to use as a border, hedge, or even as a screen. It offers attractive colorful foliage year-round and is easily cared for. While Japanese Ternstroemia can be used in full sun, it is better suited for shaded locations. The leaves can discolor somewhat during the winter in full sun. It does need a well-drained soil, and will not respond well to poorly-drained wet soils. While the plant is relatively drought-tolerant once established, it prefers regular watering.

Height: 8–20 feet • Spread: 5–6 feet • Sun: full sun to shade (shade performance is often better than in full sun) • Moisture: regular watering • Hardiness Zone: 7–9 (10) • Heat Zone: 6–10 • Propagation: seeds are the primary form of propagation; cuttings should be taken in late summer

Viburnums

Viburnum spp.

Viburnums are becoming almost as popular as azaleas, camellias, and hydrangeas. With over 120 species and numerous varieties, they have taken on a role worthy of a book unto themselves. Dr. Dirr, along with others of horticultural note, is said to be in the process of writing a book just on Viburnums. If this book ever makes its way to garden bookshelves, then Viburnums will assuredly turn the "big three" into the "big four."

For many gardeners in the south, Viburnums remain a plant in discovery, while our northern neighbors are well acquainted with them. Since they're making their way into the majority of home landscapes, we have chosen three Viburnums worthy as *Some Like It Hot* plants. We hope that we have not offended any Viburnum aficionados by excluding a favorite. However, this omission is not from a lack of affection but a lack of space, just like our landscapes.

Awabuki Viburnum

V. awabuki

Awabuki Viburnum
Viburnum awabuki

The Awabuki Viburnum is often confused with other Viburnums, especially *V. odoratissimum* and Japanese Viburnum (*V. japonica*). However, they are all separate plants. Although Awabuki Viburnum is a relative of Japanese Viburnum, and their names are often used synonymously, it is far superior in appearance. The lustrous glossy leaves are long and narrow. They are thickly arranged on the branches, which creates a solid mass of shiny dark green. The growth habit is very upright and pyramidal. The plant can get quite large—10–20 feet tall, but often stays in the 10–15 foot range. A specimen of true beauty can be seen to the left of the 10th hole at Augusta National Golf Course in Augusta, Georgia.

Much of the resurgence of this Viburnum can be attributed to the work of the late Dr. J. C. Raulston of North Carolina State University. His efforts at reintroducing this plant to the horticultural trade have resulted in an upswing of its use in landscapes throughout the southeast.

Awabuki Viburnum's attractive white flowers appear in early summer. The flower alone is enough reason to own this plant. However, the fruit that follows is even more appealing. The berries are red and begin to attract attention in late summer. The Awabuki Viburnum needs a pollinator to have good fruit set. We suggest using any of the other summer-blooming Viburnums. Awabuki Viburnum also needs a well-drained soil and protection from winter winds. Avoid wet sites for this plant.

Use Awabuki Viburnum as a specimen plant or in a shrub border. The variety 'Chindo' was introduced by Dr. Raulston after he discovered it on a trip to Chindo Island, Korea. Known for its long pendulous red berries, it is currently the predominant Awabuki Viburnum in the trade.

Height: 10–15 feet (20 feet is possible) • Spread: 4–6 feet • Sun: sun or shade • Moisture: drought-tolerant once established • Hardiness Zone: (7) 8–9 • Heat Zone: 7–10 • Propagation: stem cuttings taken from midsummer

Chinese Snowball Viburnum
V. macrocephalum

Chinese Snowball Viburnum (CSV) is a plant with such "Wow!" power that we simply could not leave it out. American gardeners have readily embraced this Chinese native.

Chinese
Snowball Viburnum
Viburnum macrocephalum

Although CSV is noted for its massive springtime flower show with a similar encore in the fall, this plant is beautiful in its own right without flowers. CSV will reach 15–20 feet tall in *Some Like It Hot* gardens. It has a rounded growth habit that spreads 10–15 feet in width. The leaves are light green and 2–4 inches long. The flowers look like a mophead hydrangea's. They are a round ball, 4–8 inches across. They begin with a greenish hue, but quickly turn to a snowball white. The flowering period lasts as long as six weeks, which carries it into the early summer in many *Some Like It Hot* gardens.

CSV does best in full sun, but it will tolerate some shade. In AHS Zones 8–10, it is probably best to offer it afternoon shade. Use a well-drained soil with moderate fertility. If the plant gets out of hand, prune it immediately after flowering. However, be forewarned that in most *Some Like It Hot* gardens, the following spring's new growth will not provide flowers. Like Mophead and Lacecap Hydrangeas, CSV blooms on second-year wood.

Height: 12–20 feet • Spread: 10–15 feet • Sun: full sun to afternoon shade, depending on heat zone • Moisture: regular watering • Hardiness Zone: 6–9 • Heat Zone: 5–10 • Propagation: softwood cuttings taken in midsummer

Sandankwa
Viburnum
V. suspensum

Sandankwa Viburnum

V. suspensum

The Sandankwa Viburnum is used mostly along the coastal regions of South Carolina to Florida. It has terrific drought tolerance and loves sandy soils. This Viburnum is capable of reaching 12 feet, and grows in almost every landscape situation. It can be used as a specimen plant, a screen, and even as a hedge plant. It is one tough hombre. As with most Viburnums, the leaves on Sandankwa Viburnum are broad and leathery. The small flowers appear in early spring and are difficult to see. The flower buds are borne on the previous season's growth, so maintaining it as a hedge will eliminate flowering unless pruning is postponed until blooming ends. The berries that appear in late summer are conspicuous. They begin red, then, as they mature, turn black by fall.

The Sandankwa Viburnum is best used in hotter AHS Zones of 8–11. It can tolerate full sun, shade, dry soil, and heat. Once it is established, this plant can be used almost anywhere without worry.

Height: 6–12 feet • Spread: 4–8 feet • Sun: full sun or shade • Moisture: drought-tolerant • Hardiness Zone: 8–9 • Heat Zone: 7–11 • Propagation: easily propagated from softwood cuttings taken in summer and hardwood cuttings taken in winter

Chaste Tree

Vitex agnus-castus

The Chaste Tree is a plant that is growing in popularity because of its ability to withstand hostile conditions while delivering blooms from summer through fall. The mature size of the Chaste Tree will depend on your USDA Zone. In Zone 6, the plant is a herbaceous perennial; in Zone 7, it is a large shrub; and in Zones 8 and higher, it can become a small tree.

The leaves are palmate, with five to seven leaflets arising from the petiole. The plant has a rounded growth habit. The flowers begin to emerge in midsummer on lilac to purple-colored stalks. The flowers will continue to develop as the summer and fall progress and as flowers are borne on new growth. Removing the spent flowers will increase the development of new buds. A large specimen in full flower is a showstopper and is a welcome attraction in any garden with room for it. While the Chaste Tree is often left to become a small tree in some landscapes, it can be pruned each year to keep it in bounds or just to maintain the shape.

Chaste Tree needs a well-drained soil in order to prosper. However, once it is established, it becomes very drought-tolerant and will accept a wide range of soils. The best location is full sun. It will even prosper in brutal western exposures. This plant is native to southern Europe and western Asia, where it is often used as a small tree.

Salina's Pink
Chaste Tree
Vitex agnus-castus

Chaste Tree
Vitex agnus-castus

Chaste Tree
Vitex agnus-castus

White forms are available, although they are purported to be less vigorous than the purple-flowering forms. Pink varieties have been available, but with disappointing results for many gardeners. A recent introduction, 'Salina's Pink' is a pink-flowering Chaste Tree that has better vigor and more consistent pink flower color than previous varieties.

Height: 6–15 feet • Spread: 8–10 feet • Sun: full sun • Moisture: drought-tolerant • Hardiness Zone: (6) 7–9 • Heat Zone: 7–10 • Propagation: seeds germinate readily. Stem cuttings taken before flowers appear do best. Hardwood cuttings taken in early winter

How the Chaste Tree Got Its Name

Vitex agnus-castus has had a long association with religious festivals and feminine purity, but when one thinks about it, the name Chaste Tree is pretty silly. Brian wondered how this common name originated and began collecting snippets of information about its scientific name, not to mention some rather peculiar customs and beliefs associated with this plant. In the meantime, P.J. got permission from the Charleston Library Society to look at their 1747 edition of Philip Miller's *The Gardener's Dictionary*. We think his explanation of *V. agnus-castus's* name is the best. It's certainly the most amusing:

> *The seeds, from the time of Dioscorides and Pliny, have been highly celebrated for securing chastity, hence the absurd official name of the shrub,* Agnus castus*; kaqarós [catharos] in Greek being the same with* castus *in Latin… Hence the Athenian matrons, in the sacred rites of Ceres, used to strew their couches with the leaves. Hence, it has had the affected name of Piper eunuchorum and monachorum.*
>
> *The seeds of the Chaste-tree are, however, so far from being thought anti-aphrodisiac, that writers of later times have ascribed to them an opposite quality; their aromatic pungency seems to favor this opinion, and Bergius states them to be carminative [induces the expulsion of gas] and emmenagogue [brings about or speeds up menstrual flow].*

While some current research suggests that *Vitex* might be useful as an herbal medicine for Premenstrual Syndrome, nothing indicates that it reduces sexual desire.

Large Shrubs and Small/ Patio Trees

Large shrubs and small/patio trees are plants that can grow big enough to achieve tree status. In the previous chapters, we proposed plants which provide some form of color during the hot and humid summer. Here, our final selection is about accent.

Southern Sugar Maple
Acer barbatum

hile we find them useful in containers on patios and decks, we cannot think of a landscape setting that does not need at least one small tree. Not every landscape has one, but if you examine a site with a critical eye, you will soon discover a spot where a small tree would benefit the overall view of the setting. Large shrubs and small trees make excellent investments. Once they are established, they have few requirements. All they ask is to be given enough room to gracefully reach their maximum growth.

Southern Sugar Maple, Florida Maple

Acer barbatum

There are three plants that Yankees can't seem to part with when they move south—lilacs, peonies, and sugar maples. With very rare exceptions, lilacs and peonies simply refuse to bloom in the deep south. They need an extended resting period in cold temperatures, which is something that's noticeably missing in most *Some Like It Hot* gardens. Consequently, they don't have enough time to gather the needed energy to bloom. Sugar maples are even more fragile. They simply won't survive in extended periods of heat and humidity. However, we offer the following horticultural solution.

The Southern Sugar Maple is a variant of the true sugar maple (*A. saccharum*). It is much more tolerant of heat than the true sugar maple, and is one of only two "sugar" maples that are viable for the AHS Zones 8 and higher. The Southern Sugar Maple will grow to 20–30 feet, but has been known to reach 60 feet. Its growth habit is more rounded than the traditional sugar maple, and its fall leaf color is yellow to orange.

A. barbatum is native throughout the southeast as an understory tree in wet areas. It is seen more often along the coastal regions than the Chalkbark Maple (*A. leucoderme*). Although it can be difficult to find in nurseries,

Southern Sugar Maple makes a nice specimen tree in the home landscape. Its fall color, something that is often absent in warm climates, makes it worth the effort to locate. When used in a *Some Like It Hot* garden, the Southern Sugar Maple can be grown in full sun or shade. Space should be given for its height and spread, which is 10–20 feet. It also makes a nice patio shade tree by providing shade in the summer and a splash of fall color that can be enjoyed while reclining on the deck. Southern Sugar Maple will lose its leaves in the winter, allowing sun to pass through it and warm the patio or deck area. This is a welcome feature when sitting on the deck in the winter.

Height: 20–30 feet • Spread: 10–20 feet • Sun: full sun or shade • Moisture: drought-tolerant once established • Hardiness Zone 7–9 • Heat Zone: 6–10 • Propagation: difficult to propagate; cuttings taken in summer have best success.

Chalkbark Maple

Acer leucoderme

Chalkbark Maple is another variant of the sugar maple which is very similar in appearance to the Southern Sugar Maple. Its distinguishing characteristic is that Chalkbark Maple has green upper and lower leaf surfaces, while the Southern Sugar Maple has a glaucous or grayish-green waxy coating that easily rubs off on the underside of the leaf. The Chalkbark Maple is native to the North Carolina Piedmont, Georgia, and the Florida panhandle. It is seen more often than the Southern Sugar Maple along the inland regions of the south-

Some Like It Hot Large Shrubs and Small/Patio Trees	
Acer barbatum	Southern Sugar Maple, Florida Maple
A. leucoderme	Chalkbark Maple
Callistemon viminalis	Weeping Bottlebrush
Citrus spp.	Citrus
C. limoni varieties	Meyer Lemon
	Lisbon Lemon
Fortunella spp.	Kumquat
× *Citrofortunella mitus*	Calamondin
Ilex × *attenuata* varieties	'East Palatka', East Palatka Holly
	'Fosters 2', Foster Holly
	'Humes', Humes Holly
	'Savannah', Savannah Holly
Koelreuteria bipinnata	Chinese Flame Tree
Lagerstroemia spp.	Crepe Myrtles
Magnolia grandiflora 'Little Gem'	Little Gem Magnolia
Ulmus parvifolia	Chinese Lacebark Elm

east coast. It will get 20–30 feet tall and 10–20 feet wide. It is very tolerant of dry soils and is almost always found in the wild as an understory tree. The fall colors are yellow, orange, and red. Like the Southern Sugar Maple, Chalkbark Maple performs well in full sun or shade and can be used in the same manner. It has better cold-hardiness than the Southern Sugar Maple, which makes it is a better choice for USDA Zones too cold for Southern Sugar Maple, but too hot for good sugar maple growth.

Height: 20–30 feet • Spread: 10–20 feet • Sun: full sun to shade • Moisture: drought-tolerant once established • Hardiness Zone: 5–9 • Heat Zone: 4–10 • Propagation: difficult to propagate; cuttings taken in summer have best success.

Citrus

Citrus spp.
× *Citrofortunella mitis*
Fortunella spp.

Many readers, especially those who garden in USDA Zone 9b and further south, are probably wondering why we have a section on citrus. After all, one hearty freeze will kill most of these plants. This means that many *Some Like It Hot* gardeners are faced with lugging potted citrus indoors whenever killing temperatures are predicted. If the plants can't be moved, creative emergency measures must be devised. We have seen some gallant efforts—some worked while others were silly and destined to failure.

Regardless of the inconvenience, the annual ritual of trying to save these tropical plants from inevitable temperature crashes is something that diehard citrus aficionados accept. Dooryard or home garden citrus growing is becoming increasingly popular, and garden centers throughout the southeast are trying to meet the demands of enthusiastic collectors. Because some citrus trees have lower freeze thresholds than others (we are splitting hairs here, but a degree or two can make a world of difference), we have selected only a few that most *Some Like It Hot* gardeners can enjoy. But before we introduce you to the calamondin (× *Citrofortunella mitis*), the kumquat (*Fortunella* spp.), and two lemon cultivars (*Citrus limoni*), we return to citrus in general.

We have noticed that owning citrus plants frequently drives perfectly sane gardeners to fits of irrationality. This is unfortunate, because these evergreen, wonderfully aromatic plants are relatively easy to grow, notwithstanding the obligatory three days near the end of winter when it suddenly gets colder than Alaska. We hope the following information will calm the anxious.

The most frequently asked question about citrus goes something like this: "I stuck an orange (or grapefruit) seed in a pot and it sprouted. When can I expect fruit?" The answer is simple: Don't expect fruit for about ten years. However, chances are that you'll start to have doubts about your shiny, dark-green seedling long before you're given the opportunity to be disappointed with the fruit. Indeed, we suspect that most people toss out their plant long before the possibility of fruiting.

The problem is that citrus seeds do not breed true. In fact, most varieties hybridize so easily that taxonomists continually go nuts over citrus classifications. When a seed doesn't breed true, it simply means that the fruit will be different from the parent plant's. Of course, the next question is: "Then how did we get the plants we have now?" Because it is our wont never to leave things alone, man began tinkering thousands of years ago with citrus. He wanted to improve the juice. Somewhere along the line, he discovered that stem cuttings and grafts were the only ways to propagate identical copies of his favorite citrus.

Of course, every now and then, someone raises a citrus from seed and is lucky enough to get a desirable plant. We know of a woman in Charleston who did just that. However, ninety-nine percent of the seeds you plant will turn out to be an unmitigated bust. In addition to the painfully long wait for a dis-pleasing fruit, the plant's overall unattractive traits can't be ignored. While many citrus have thorns, trees planted from seed are excessively thorny. Their shape is often unruly and pruning doesn't help. So, what does one do with a seed-grown citrus? Use its rootstock for grafting a desirable cultivar.

We have also discovered that folks get anxious about citrus's soil require-ments. The general assumption is that these plants need lots of sand and a very low pH. That's probably because people in the southeast associate citrus with the Gulf Coast's sandy soils. However, citrus will thrive even in clay soils if the drainage is good. Citrus is nonchalant about pH too. Although a pH between 5.5 and 6.5 is often recommended, they will do just fine in slightly sweeter soils, up to a pH of 8. Use a balanced fertilizer. If your plant comes with grow-ing instructions on the tag, save it and follow the grower's recommendations. When citrus leaves begin to look light green or yellowish, spray chelated iron on the leaves or apply a liquid fertilizer specially formulated for acid-loving plants. They, too, contain chelated iron.

Citrus is easy to maintain after the first year. Planting should be done in the spring or very early summer. Make sure it is planted slightly elevated to the ground line and placed in well-drained soil. This will protect the plant from crown and/or root rot. Citrus trees need high temperatures to bear fruit, so it is necessary to get them settled and blooming as fast as possible. Anticipate extra watering during the hot summer months until they are established. Remember too that, as a defense, citrus leaves will droop in the heat of the day. Overreacting to this phenomenon is common, so we recommend using a mois-ture meter. Too much water leads to root rot.

If you have a micro-environment in your garden that offers a protected southern exposure with about six hours of summer sunlight, then growing a Meyer lemon, kumquat, or calamondin in the ground is a realistic suggestion. (We have admired a 10-foot tall calamondin snuggled up in an alley near the Charleston Harbor for years.) For the really bold, try a Lisbon lemon. This cultivar is a little more susceptible to the cold than the Meyer.

Kumquats and calamondins are both *Fortunella* species. They are quite hearty and make splendid ornamental plants. P.J.'s thirteen-year-old potted calamondin has been subjected to all sorts of horticultural indignities—including being pot-bound, not given enough water, and deprived of fertilizer—yet it continues to produce hundreds of quarter-size "oranges" each year. If you enjoy the oval-shaped kumquat (*F. margarita* 'Nagami') from your grocer's produce section, then we also recommend growing the rounder-fruited 'Meiwa' (*F. japonica*).

We think dooryard citrus can add interest and a bit of novelty to the home landscape. We have offered only a few varieties that we are confident will survive in most southern yards. However, if a reputable garden center or nursery near you offers a cultivar that we have not mentioned, read the tag carefully, ask questions if you have any doubts, and then enjoy your purchase.

Height: 8–20 feet (dwarf varieties 3–10 feet; semi-dwarf 6–18 feet) • Spread: up to 20 feet for standard varieties • Sun: full sun • Moisture: regular moisture • Hardiness Zone: 8–10 • Heat Zone: 1–12 • Propagation: Meyer lemon is one of the few citrus cultivars that can be successfully propagated from stem cuttings. All others are grafted. Rootstock may be grown from seed

Calamondin
× *Citrofortunella mitis*

Weeping Bottlebrush

Callistemon viminalis

Weeping Bottlebrush is another one of those "Wow!" plants. The branches and flowers on this 20–25 foot tree hang straight down like a weeping mulberry or cherry. The visual impact of flowers hanging upside down is amazing. If you are familiar with the shrubby forms of bottlebrush, then you can imagine the impression a small tree that's completely covered with red bottlebrush-like flowers makes. We can't say enough about this tree's form or the statement it has in a landscape. 'Red Cascade' is a noteworthy variety of Weeping Bottlebrush. The first time Brian saw one was at the Henry P. Leu Garden in Orlando, Florida. The tree was in the parking lot, of all places, and was in full bloom in early February. As with many of the bottlebrush species, this plant is only

Weeping Bottlebrush
Callistemon viminalis

East Palatka Holly
Ilex × attenuata

cold-hardy in USDA Zones 9 and higher. So the majority of *Some Like It Hot* gardeners will have to visit Florida and south Texas to see this tree.

Height: 20–25 feet, except compact forms 4 feet • Spread: 10–15 feet • Sun: full sun • Moisture: regular watering • Hardiness Zone: 9–11 • Heat Zone: 8–12 • Propagation: unknown

Holly

Ilex × attenuata varieties

All of these holly varieties were developed from the same parents. Dahoon Holly (*Ilex cassine*) was crossed with American Holly (*I. opaca*) to create these hybrids, and all of their offspring are well suited for *Some Like It Hot* gardens. These plants make nice tree accents and they are good substitutes for evergreens like junipers that don't always take the heat of warmer climates.

'East Palatka', East Palatka Holly

Fosters Holly
Ilex × attenuata

'East Palatka' was a seedling discovered in the wild near East Palatka, Florida in 1927. The plant will grow to about 20–30 feet tall and spread 15–20 feet wide. It has a more airy growth habit than other cultivars of this kind of holly, but the leaves are still dark green and you can expect a profusion of red berries in the fall. The leaves are 2–3 inches long and 1–2 inches wide.

'Fosters 2', Fosters Holly

'Fosters 2' is a very narrow leaf form. The leaves are $1^1/_2$–2 inches long and only 1 inch wide. They have a distinct spine pattern of one or more spines at the tip of the leaf. It has the darkest green leaf of these hollies. It will grow 20–30 feet high and makes a thick, tall shrub or small tree, depending on how it is pruned.

'Humes', Humes Holly

The 'Humes' produces a more rounded leaf form than its relatives. The leaves are medium green and contrast well with the very bright red berries that appear in the fall. This plant grows into a rounded form, which makes a nice large shrub/tree. We are familiar with a specimen growing on the campus of Trident Technical College in North Charleston, South Carolina. It is a beautiful plant, with branches draping all the way down to the ground. The berries make it even more attractive.

'Savannah', Savannah Holly

The 'Savannah' is, by any account, the most popular of the *Ilex × attenuata* varieties. 'Savannah' is known for its ability to perform well in wet sites. It was discovered just outside of Savannah, Georgia in the late 1960s. The leaves are broad and share a close resemblance in size and spine arrangement to its American Holly parent. However, its distinguishing characteristic is the petiole-to-tip V-shaped leaf. The leaves are a lighter, almost pale, green and the shrub produces nice berries in the fall. The growth habit is more pyramidal than the other hollies mentioned above.

Height: 20–30 feet • Spread: 10–20 feet • Sun: full sun or light shade • Moisture: drought-tolerant • Hardiness Zone: 7–9 • Heat Zone: 6–9 • Propagation: stem cuttings taken in the fall

Chinese Flame Tree
Koelreuteria bipinnata

This is Brian's favorite late-summer-flowering tree. The Chinese Flame Tree is a moderately fast-growing small tree that reaches heights of 20–30 feet. The leaves have a tropical look and the plant takes on a vase-shaped appearance once it gets some size. The flowers will appear in August when almost nothing else is in flower. The 1–2 foot long panicles of bright yellow flowers emerge at the end of new growth and cover the tree in a fabulous display. However, the best is yet to come each year. The flowers fade in a few weeks, and by October, pink papery seedpods form, which create an even bigger spectacle than the flowers. The seedpods hold their color for several weeks. If collected

Humes Holly
Ilex × attenuata

Savannah Holly
Ilex × attenuata

Chinese Flame Tree
Koelreuteria bipinnata

at the peak of their color, they can be displayed as a dried arrangement for several weeks with their vibrant color holding through Christmas or longer.

Chinese Flame Tree is very tolerant of soil types, and can handle full sun or shade. This makes it a good choice for use as a specimen plant or as part of a cover for shade-tolerant shrubs. It reproduces profusely from seed, and in some states is considered a noxious weed. Therefore, before including it in your landscape, check with local experts. It is native to China.

Height: 20–30 feet • Spread: 10–15 feet • Sun: full sun or shade • Moisture: regular watering, but drought-tolerant once established • Hardiness Zone: 6–9 • Heat Zone: 5–10 • Propagation: easily reproduced from seeds

Crepe Myrtle

Lagerstroemia spp.

The Crepe Myrtle is the quintessential summer small-flowering tree. The work done by several breeders, including Carl Whitcomb, the late Don Egolf, and his successor Margaret Pooler, has produced a plethora of colors, shapes, sizes, and bark color for gardeners to choose from. Unfortunately, only a small handful of varieties are commonly used. This is unfortunate because, if there is a specific need, there is a Crepe Myrtle to fit the requirement. This of course, leads us to that tragic ritual—the wanton butchering of these plants each spring.

"Crepe murder" is often committed to reduce plant height. Because home gardeners have been unaware that shorter varieties are available, many resort to whacking back their plants when they grow too tall. Then, after someone came up with the silly idea that a Bart-Simpson-style flattop would increase flowering, everyone—including landscaping services—began performing crepe murder. The flattops-are-good myth has been dispelled through the work of various professionals, most notably City of Charlotte Urban Forester Laura Brewer. She has demonstrated that when Crepe Myrtles are lightly pruned or left untouched, they flower sooner and with more profusion than do levelled-off plants. If you have a Crepe Myrtle that is too tall for its site, the answer is not to continue severe pruning each spring. Instead, turn to the numerous varieties on the market and choose one that suits your height requirement.

Crepe Myrtles will not perform well in wet sites or in deep shade. When selecting a site, look for full sun—up to 6–8 hours per day—and a well-drained soil with moderate fertility. Fertilization in poor soils boosts the plant's fullness, but is not necessary in other settings.

A commonly asked question is why a specific Crepe Myrtle will not flower. The answer is almost always a lack of sunlight. While Crepe Myrtles will remain healthy looking in part-day sun, flower production will be reduced or nonexistent.

Another frequently asked question is how does one get rid of powdery mildew (*Erysiphe lagerstroemia*). While proper pruning practices will help keep a tree healthy, and therefore less vulnerable to disease, we suggest that you plant varieties that are resistant to powdery mildew.

We are including a table with information on Crepe Myrtle varieties that are resistant to powdery mildew, as well as other important facts. Paul Thompson, York County Clemson Extension Horticulture Agent, created this chart and we are grateful that he agreed to share it with *Some Like It Hot* readers. You may also want to visit the Crepe Myrtle Varieties home page, of which Brian and Paul are co-authors, on the Internet at www.clemson.edu/crepemyrtle.

National Arboretum and Dr. Don Egolf

The world of Crepe Myrtles is one of endless varieties. Some Crepe Myrtle cultivar—with almost any flower color you desire—can be found for practically any situation you have. However, this was not the case a few decades ago. The National Arboretum in Washington, DC has been the focal point of Crepe Myrtle development for the last half-century. It started in the late 1950s with Dr. Don Egolf, Research Horticulturist at the Arboretum. Dr. Egolf noticed that Japanese Crepe Myrtles (*L. fauriei*) did not have powdery mildew, which is a common disease problem on Indica Crepe Myrtles (*L. indica*). He theorized that by crossing the two species, new varieties could be produced that would have the Indica's splendid flower colors, the notable trunk characteristics of the Japanese, and be resistant to powdery mildew.

The result revolutionized the Crepe Myrtle industry and led to their widespread use that we continue to enjoy today. Dr. Egolf's work, and that of his successor, Dr. Margaret Pooler, has resulted in the introduction of over thirty varieties of Crepe Myrtle from the National Arboretum. The amazing thing—and a true testament to the program's success—is that not only did varieties with different flower color and powdery mildew resistance come about, but varying mature heights, growth habit, and bark characteristics also emerged. Dr. Egolf developed other varieties of plants as well, but none of those accomplishments equalled his work in new Crepe Myrtle varieties.

One of the reasons the National Arboretum's breeding program is so successful is the rigorous evaluation program that each plant goes through before it is named and released to the industry. It begins with the first year a Crepe Myrtle is grown from seed. If it shows any susceptibility to powdery mildew, it is thrown on the trash pile. In fact, throughout the evaluation program, if a plant is seen to be regularly infected it is discarded and dropped from the program. After several years of evaluating the pest resistance of the new plants, those with good or useful traits are selected. Then a series of trials is conducted all across the U.S. with cooperators, like land grant universities, to see how these potential cultivars perform in different areas. If it fails in one or several geographical areas, it is dropped from the program. While this may seem like an unnecessarily strict standard to some, the results cannot be argued with. Each Crepe Myrtle that is finally released will work anywhere in the U.S. that can grow them.

The fact that such a high standard is used, and the number of varieties that have been released, speak volumes about the commitment of the National Arboretum's breeding program. For every Crepe Myrtle variety you see with an Indian tribe name attached to it, thousands of Crepe Myrtle seedlings were germinated, cared for, shared with cooperators and thrown on the trash pile.

Crepe Myrtle Varieties (Source: Paul Thompson, Clemson Extension Service)

Variety	Type	Height	Flower Color	Flowering Period	Growth Habit	Fall Color	Bark Color	Powd. Mildew Resistance
DWARF - 5 FEET OR LESS								
Chickasaw	hybrid	3+	lavender pink	90 days	dwarf	bronze red	n/a	very good
Firecracker	indica	3–5	light red	100 days	dwarf	red orange	n/a	very good
Ozark Spring	indica	3–5+	lavender	70 days	dwarf	yellow	gray-brown	very good
Pocomoke	hybrid	to 3	rose pink	80 days	compact mound	bronze red	n/a	very good
Velma's Royal Delight	indica	3–5+	magenta	75 days	upright	light maroon	light gray	good
Victor	indica	3–4	red	85 days	compact	yellow	n/a	moderate
SEMI-DWARF - 5–10 FEET								
Acoma	hybrid	5–10+	white	90 days	spreading	purple red	cream, tan gray	very good
Caddo	hybrid	5–10+	bright pink	80 days	spreading	orange red	gray, light cinnamon	very good
Hopi	hybrid	5–10+	medium pink	100 days	spreading	orange red	tan, cream	very good
Pecos	hybrid	5–10	medium pink	80 days	semi-dwarf	maroon	tan, dark cinnamon	very good
Prairie Lace	indica	5–10	pink w/white edges	90 days	compact upright	red	tan, gray	very good
Tonto	hybrid	5–10+	red	75 days	globose	bright maroon	cream, light chestnut	very good
Zuni	hybrid	5–10+	lavender	100 days	globose	red orange	tan, taupe white	very good
SMALL TREE - 10–20 FEET								
Byer's Regal Red	indica	10–20	dark red	70 days	broad upright	red orange	gray, tan	very good
Catawba	indica	10–20	purple	70 days	globose	red orange	gray-brown	good

Crepe Myrtle Varieties (continued)

Variety	Type	Height	Flower Color	Flowering Period	Growth Habit	Fall Color	Bark Color	Powd. Mildew Resistance
SMALL TREE - 10–20 FEET (continued)								
Centennial Spirit	indica	10–20	electric red	95 days	upright	red orange	mottled gray cream, taupe	fair
Comanche	hybrid	10–15	coral pink	80 days	broad upright	red	light sandlewood	very good
Conestoga	indica	10–20	lavender	70 days	broad, open, arch	yellow bronze	light gray-brown	moderate
Country Red	indica	10–20	red	60–70 days	upright	orange	cream, taupe	very good
Lipan	hybrid	10–20	lavender	80 days	broad upright	orange to red	gray, beige white	very good
Osage	hybrid	10–20	light pink	100 days	spreading pendulous	red	mottled gray, dark chestnut	very good
Powhatan	indica	10–20	lavender	75 days	spreading	yellow orange	light gray-brown	very good
Raspberry Sundae	indica	10–20	red w/ white edges		upright columnar		gray-brown	moderate
Royal Velvet	indica	10–20	bright pink	120 days	spreading	orange	gray-brown	good
Seminole	indica	10–20	medium pink	75 days	globose	yellow, red	gray, taupe	good
Sioux	hybrid	10–20	dark pink	90 days	narrow upright	maroon	gray, tan, brown	very good
William Toovey	indica	10–20	dark pink	90 days	broad vase	red orange	light gray-brown	good
Yuma	hybrid	10–20	lavender	90 days	upright	yellow orange	light pinkish-orange, tan	very good
MEDIUM TREE - 20–30 FEET								
Apalachee	hybrid	15–20	light lavender	90 days	upright vase	russet	chestnut, beige, taupe	very good

Crepe Myrtle Varieties (continued)

Variety	Type	Height	Flower Color	Flowering Period	Growth Habit	Fall Color	Bark Color	Powd. Mildew Resistance
MEDIUM TREE - 20–30 FEET (continued)								
Byer's Hardy Lavender	indica	20+	lavender	75 days	broad upright vase	red	gray, pinkish-tan	good
Byer's Wonderful White	indica	20+	white	80 days	broad	yellow	gray, tan	good
Choctaw	hybrid	25–30	bright pink	90 days	globose	maroon	tan, chestnut	very good
Dallas Red	indica	20+	red	70 days	upright vase		cream, taupe	good
Dynamite	indica	20+	deep red	100 days	broad vase	orange	gray-brown	very good
Miami	hybrid	25+	dark coral	100 days	upright vase	orange	tan, bright rust	very good
Muskogee	hybrid	25–30	light lavender	120 days	broad upright	red orange	gray, pinkish-brown	very good
Potomac	indica	20+	medium pink	90 days	upright vase	orange	light gray-brown	very good
Red Rocket	indica	20+	bright red	100 days	upright	red orange	gray-brown	very good
Sarah's Favorite	hybrid	20+	white		broad spreading	red	tan, gray, cinnamon	very good
Townhouse	fauriei	20+	white	70 days	speading	orange yellow	exfoliating dark brown	good
Tuscarora	hybrid	20+	dark coral pink	70 days	broad vase	red orange	tan, gray, light brown	good
Tuskegee	hybrid	20+	dark pink	100 days	broad spreading	red orange	beige, tan gray	good
Wichita	hybrid	25+	lavender	110 days	upright vase	cooper	tan, mottled mahogany	very good

Crepe Myrtle Varieties (continued)

Variety	Type	Height	Flower Color	Flowering Period	Growth Habit	Fall Color	Bark Color	Powd. Mildew Resistance
LARGE TREE - 30 FEET OR GREATER								
Basham's Party Pink	hybrid	to 35	lavender pink	80 days	broad upright	orange yellow	beige, taupe	good
Biloxi	hybrid	25–30	pale pink	80 days	upright vase	yellow to red	tan, dark chestnut	very good
Fantasy	fauriei	35+	white	70 days	upright vase	yellow	dark red to rusty brown	very good
Fauriei	fauriei	20–35+	white	70–90 days	broad vase	variable	tan, dark cinnamon to mahogany	very good
Kiowa	fauriei	30+	white	90 days	broad vase	red orange	tan, brilliant cinnamon	very good
Natchez	hybrid	20–35+	white	110 days	arching vase	red orange	cream, dark cinnamon	very good

The heights indicated in this chart are what is to be expected after 10–15 years. With the exception of the true dwarf varieties, there is no indication from research that growth will cease in the warmer climates of Zones 8–10.

Little Gem Magnolia
Magnolia grandiflora
'Little Gem'

Little Gem Magnolia

Magnolia grandiflora 'Little Gem'

Nothing quite equals the smell of Southern Magnolia (*Magnolia grandiflora*) blossoms on a warm, humid summer evening. If you have no room for such a magnificent plant, then consider the 'Little Gem'. The introduction of this smaller version of the grandiflora has opened up new avenues for home gardeners with limited space. This is a plant that is gaining in popularity and rightfully so.

Although 'Little Gem' can reach 20 feet in height, its smaller size makes it a feasible doorway tree. It can also be espaliered. Unlike its big brother, it is a quick starter and will begin flowering during the first year. The lemon-fragrant blossoms are irresistible when they open in early summer. 'Little Gem' will also flower much later into the fall than the traditional Southern Magnolia.

'Little Gem' will do best in sites where it receives full sun. Flowering may be reduced if placed in too much shade. The soil should be well drained, but avoid planting in dry spots.

'Teddy Bear' is an even newer selection of Southern Magnolia. Introduced by Bob and Bill Head of Head-Lee Nursery in Seneca, South Carolina, it is a dwarf type like 'Little Gem'. It is more compact in its growth habit with additional density coming from the tighter spacing between leaves.

Height: 15–20 feet • Spread: 5–10 feet • Sun: full sun • Moisture: regular watering • Hardiness Zone: 7–9 • Heat Zone: 6–9 • Propagation: easiest of the Southern Magnolias to propagate. Use softwood cuttings

Chinese Lacebark Elm

Ulmus parvifolia

Chinese Lacebark Elm is a woefully underutilized tree although it is finally gaining some popularity. That's good news because it may be the best urban street tree available. It can take the cruelest conditions (hot pavements and wet, compacted soils) and is resilient against all pests including Dutch elm disease. Although this Chinese native can grow 70–80 feet tall, the mature height differs among varieties. The small dark green elliptical leaves are closely spaced, which gives the tree a very full canopy.

Little Gem Magnolia
Magnolia grandiflora
'Little Gem'

Chinese Lacebark Elm
Ulmus parvifolia
'Allee' ®

Chinese Lacebark Elm bears flowers in late summer, just when temperatures begin to hint that the brutal heat of summer is ending. The winged fruit, reminiscent of maple seeds, begins to fall by late September. Its bark may be the tree's most attractive feature. Even on smaller, 1–2 inch caliper trees, the bark takes on a lacy pattern of light brown, gray, green, and orange.

Chinese Lacebark Elm is a wonderful tree for any *Some Like It Hot* garden. The plant's form and color, not to mention its splendid bark, make it a beautiful accent tree. These magnificent traits make it a true "poster child" for the species. Vickery's, a restaurant in downtown Charleston, has an exceptional specimen that shades the outdoor dining area.

Although Chinese Lacebark Elm performs best in well-drained soils that receive regular moisture, it will thrive during summer's fickle spells of dry or wet. Because it has very little root area, this tree can tolerate sun, shade, and a wide range of soil conditions.

When selecting a Chinese Lacebark Elm, the most important consideration is a variety that is appropriately sized for your site. Allee® is an upright growing form that can get 70 feet tall and 20–30 feet wide. Athena® is a broad, spreading form that can reach 20–40 feet tall and 50 feet wide. 'Drake' is the popular choice for those needing a small tree. Drake will grow 20–30 feet tall and 20–30 feet wide.

Height: 20–70 feet, depending on variety • Spread: 20–50 feet, depending on variety • Sun: full sun or shade • Moisture: likes regular watering, but drought-tolerant once established • Hardiness Zone: 5–9, depending on variety • Heat Zone: 4–10 • Propagation: cuttings taken in midsummer and treated with root hormone. Seeds collected fresh do not need cold treatment, but if allowed to dry, a two-month cold treatment is required.

Chinese Lacebark Elm
Ulmus parvifolia

At-a-Glance
Plant Lists

Our "At-a-Glance" lists are for folks who need quick, general information about plant attributes and their growth habits. These lists come in handy when planning for a major landscape project or when you're just trying to figure out what kind of plant will work in a particular spot.

Perhaps one of the most difficult tasks in site selection is deciding not only how much sun an area receives, but also what kind of exposure it is getting. Many of us have our own interpretation of "full sun" or "shade," which means that the best definition probably falls under the "I know it when I see it" maxim. The following guidelines might help:

Full Sun: At least 6–8 hours of direct sunlight per day.

Filtered Sun: Sunlight that shines through a canopy of trees or large shrubs. The canopy's leaves will make the light less intense in the summer.

Partial Shade: 3–5 hours of direct sunlight per day.

Light Shade: 2–3 hours of shade per day.

Shade: Less than 2 hours of direct sunlight per day.

Plants for Full Sun

Ornamental Grasses

Cortaderia selloana	Pampas Grass
Cymbopogon citratus	Lemon Grass
Imperata cylindrica rubra	Japanese Blood Grass
Miscanthus spp.	Miscanthus
Muhlenbergia capillaris	Pink Muhly Sweetgrass
M. filipes	Purple Muhly Sweetgrass
Pennisetum alopecuroides	Fountain Grass
P. setaceum rubrum	Purple Fountain Grass

Plants for Full Sun (continued)

Annual Vines

Antigonon leptopus	Coral Vine
Clitoria ternatea 'Blue Sails'	Blue Sails Vine
Cobaea scandens	Cup-and-Saucer Vine
Dolichos lablab Syn. *Lablab purpureus*	Hyacinth Bean
Ipomoea alba	Moonvine
I. tricolor	Morning Glory
I. × multifida	Cardinal Vine
Mandevilla spp.	Mandevilla
Mascagnia macroptera	Yellow Orchid Vine, Butterfly Vine
Phaseolus coccineus	Scarlet Runner Bean
Pseudogynoxys chenopodioides Syn. *Senecio confusus*	Mexican Flame Vine
Thunbergia alata	Black-Eyed Susan Vine
T. grandiflora	Blue Sky Vine, Blue Indian Vine
T. gregorii	Orange Clock Vine
Vigna (formerly *Phaseolus*) *caracalla*	Snail Vine, Caracalla Bean

Small Shrubs

Lagerstroemia hybrids	Dwarf Crepe Myrtles

Small to Medium Shrubs

Buddleia davidii	Butterfly Bush

Plants for Full Sun (continued)

Medium to Large Shrubs

Callicarpa acuminata	Mexican Beautyberry
C. acuminata 'Woodlanders'	Woodlanders Mexican Beautyberry
C. rigidus	Bottlebrush
C. viminalis 'Captain Cook'	Weeping Bottlebrush
C. viminalis 'McCaskillii'	Weeping Bottlebrush
Duranta erecta	Golden Dewdrop, Sky Flower
Illicium parviflorum	Small Anise-Tree
Indigofera amblyantha	no common name
Vitex angus-castus	Chaste Tree

Large Shrubs and Small/Patio Trees

Callistemon viminalis	Weeping Bottlebrush
Citrus limoni varieties	Meyer and Lisbon Lemon
Fortunella spp.	Kumquat
× *Citrofortunella mitis*	Calamondin
Ilex × *attenuata* varieties	Holly
Lagerstroemia spp.	Crepe Myrtles
Magnolia grandiflora 'Little Gem'	Little Gem Magnolia

Plants for Full Sun or Half-Day Shade

Ornamental Grasses

Panicum virgatum	Switch-Grass, Panic Grass

Plants for Full Sun or Half-Day Shade (continued)

Medium to Large Shrubs

Illicium parviflorum	Small Anise-Tree
Senna corymbosa formerly *Cassia corymbosa*	Flowery Senna
S. marilandica formerly *C. marilandica*	Wild Senna

Plants for Full Sun or Light Shade

Ornamental Grasses

Andropogon glomeratus	Bushy Bluestem

Medium to Large Shrubs

Illicium parviflorum	Small Anise-Tree

Large Shrubs and Small/Patio Trees

Ilex × attenuata 'East Palatka'	East Palatka Holly
I. × attenuata 'Fosters 2'	Foster Holly
I. × attenuata 'Humes'	Humes Holly
I. × attenuata 'Savannah'	Savannah Holly

Plants for Full Sun or Partial Shade

Medium to Large Shrubs

Abelia chinensis	Chinese Abelia
A. × 'Edward Goucher'	Edward Goucher Abelia
A. × *grandiflora*	Glossy Abelia
Bambusa multiplex	Clump Bamboo
Callicarpa americana	American Beautyberry
C. bodinieri 'Profusion'	Bodinier 'Profusion' Beautyberry
Illicium parviflorum	Small Anise-Tree
Loropetalum chinense var. *rubrum*	Pink Flowering Loropetalum

Plants That Prefer Full Sun to Afternoon Shade

Medium to Large Shrubs

Illicium parviflorum	Small Anise-Tree
Viburnum macrocephalum	Chinese Snowball Viburnum

Plants That Prefer Full Sun but Will Grow in Shade

Medium to Large Shrubs

Illicium parviflorum	Small Anise-Tree
Ternstroemia gymnanthera	Japanese Ternstroemia, Cleyera

Plants for Full Sun or Shade

Ornamental Grasses

Calamagrostis brachytricha	Korean Feather Reed Grass
Chasmanthium latifolium	Wild Oats, Upland Sea Oats
Liriope grandiflora	Evergreen Giant Liriope
L. muscari	Liriope
L. muscari 'Big Blue'	Big Blue Liriope
L. spicata	Creeping Lilyturf

Annual Vines

Clerodendrum splendens	Bleeding Heart Vine
Passiflora spp.	Passionflower

Small Shrubs

Aronia melanocarpa	Black Chokeberry
Gardenia augusta 'Radicans'	Dwarf Gardenia

Small to Medium Shrubs

Clethra alnifolia	Clethra, Summersweet

Plants for Full Sun or Shade (continued)

Medium to Large Shrubs

Callicarpa dichotoma	Purple Beautyberry
C. dichotoma 'Albifructus'	Purple Beautyberry 'Albifructus'
C. dichomata 'Spring Gold'	Purple Beautyberry 'Spring Gold'
Calycanthus floridus	Sweet Shrub, Carolina Allspice
Illicium floridanum	Florida Anise-Tree
I. parviflorum	Small Anise-Tree
Viburnum suspensum	Sandankwa Viburnum

Large Shrubs and Small/Patio Trees

Acer barbatum	Southern Sugar Maple, Florida Maple
A. leucoderme	Chalkbark Maple
Koelreuteria bipinnata	Chinese Flame Tree
Ulmus parvifolia	Chinese Lacebark Elm

Plants That Prefer Half-Day Shade or All-Day Filtered Sun

Medium to Large Shrubs

Illicium parviflorum	Small Anise-Tree
Stewartia monadelpha	Tall Stewartia

Plants That Prefer Part-Day to Full-Day Shade

Annual Vines

Dicentra scandens	Yellow Bleeding Heart Vine

Medium to Large Shrubs

Agarista populifolia or *Leucothoe populifolia*	Florida Leucothoe, Tall Leucothoe

Plants That Prefer Partial Shade to Shade

Medium to Large Shrubs

Illicium floridanum	Florida Anise-Tree
Rhododendron prunifolium	Plumleaf Azalea
R. serrulatum	Hammocksweet Azalea
R. viscosum	Swamp Azalea

Plants for Shade

Ornamental Grasses

Ophiopogon japonicus	Mondo Grass
O. japonicus 'Nana'	Dwarf Mondo Grass 'Nana'

Annual Vines

Aristolochia durior	Dutchman's Pipe
A. elegans	Calico Flower

Plants for Shade (continued)
Small Shrubs

Ardisia crenata	Coralberry
A. japonica	Japanese Ardisia, Marlberry
Indigofera decora	Pink Indigo

Small to Medium Shrubs

Kerria japonica	Kerria, Japanese Kerria
Mahonia bealei	Leatherleaf Mahonia
M. fortunei	Chinese Mahonia

Medium to Large Shrubs

Illicium floridanum	Florida Anise-Tree
I. parviflorum	Small Anise-Tree

Plants That Will Always Need Regular Watering
Ornamental Grasses

Carex spp.	Sedge
Cymbopogon citratus	Lemon Grass
Muhlenbergia capillaris	Pink Muhly Sweetgrass
M. filipes	Purple Muhly Sweetgrass
Pennisetum setaceum rubrum	Purple Fountain Grass

Plants That Will Always Need Regular Watering (continued)

Annual Vines

Antigonon leptopus	Coral Vine
Aristolochia durior	Dutchman's Pipe
A. elegans	Calico Flower
Clerodendrum splendens	Bleeding Heart Vine
Clitoria ternatea 'Blue Sails'	Blue Sails Vine
Cobaea scandens	Cup-and-Saucer Vine
Dicentra scandens	Yellow Bleeding Heart Vine
Dolichos lablab Syn. *Lablab purpureus*	Hyacinth Bean
Ipomoea alba	Moonvine
I. × multifida	Cardinal Vine
I. tricolor	Morning Glory
Mandevilla spp.	Mandevilla
Mascagnia macroptera	Yellow Orchid Vine, Butterfly Vine
Passiflora spp.	Passionflower
Phaseolus coccineus	Scarlet Runner Bean
Pseudogynoxys chenopodioides Syn. *Senecio confusus*	Mexican Flame Vine
Thunbergia alata	Black-Eyed Susan Vine
T. grandiflora	Blue Sky Vine, Blue Indian Vine
T. gregorii	Orange Clock Vine
Vigna (formerly *Phaseolus*) *caracalla*	Snail Vine, Caracalla Bean

Plants That Will Always Need Regular Watering (continued)

Small Shrubs

Aronia melanocarpa	Black Chokeberry

Small to Medium Shrubs

Clethra alnifolia	Clethra, Summersweet

Medium to Large Shrubs

Agarista populifolia or *Leucothoe populifolia*	Florida Leucothoe, Tall Leucothoe
Callicarpa acuminata	Mexican Beautyberry
C. acuminata 'Woodlanders'	Woodlanders Mexican Beautyberry
Callistemon viminalis 'Captain Cook'	Weeping Bottlebrush
C. viminalis 'McCaskillii'	Weeping Bottlebrush
Calycanthus floridus	Sweet Shrub, Carolina Allspice
Duranta erecta	Golden Dewdrop, Sky Flower
Hydrangea macrophylla macrophylla	Mophead Hydrangea
H. macrophylla normalis	Lacecap Hydrangea
H. quercifolia	Oakleaf Hydrangea
Indigofera amblyantha	no common name
Loropetalum chinense var. *rubrum*	Pink Flowering Loropetalum
Rhododendron serrulatum	Hammocksweet Azalea
R. viscosum	Swamp Azalea
Senna corymbosa formerly *Cassia corymbosa*	Flowery Senna

Plants That Will Always Need Regular Watering (continued)
Medium to Large Shrubs (continued)

Senna marilandica formerly *Cassia marilandica*	Wild Senna
Ternstroemia gymnanthera	Japanese Ternstroemia, Cleyera
Viburnum macrocephalum	Chinese Snowball Viburnum

Large Shrubs and Small/Patio Trees

Callistemon viminalis	Weeping Bottlebrush
Citrus limoni varieties	Meyer and Lisbon Lemon
Fortunella spp.	Kumquat
× *Citrofortunella mitis*	Calamondin
Magnolia grandiflora 'Little Gem'	Little Gem Magnolia

Plants That Need Regular Watering Until They Are Established
Ornamental Grasses

Chasmanthium latifolium	Wild Oats, Upland Sea Oats
Cortaderia selloana	Pampas Grass
Imperata cylindrica rubra	Japanese Blood Grass
Liriope grandiflora	Evergreen Giant Liriope
L. muscari	Liriope
L. muscari 'Big Blue'	Big Blue Liriope
L. spicata	Creeping Lilyturf
Miscanthus spp.	Miscanthus

Plants That Need Regular Watering Until They Are Established
(continued)

Ornamental Grasses (continued)

Ophiopogon japonicus	Mondo Grass
O. japonicus 'Nana'	Dwarf Mondo Grass 'Nana'
Pennisetum alopecuroides	Fountain Grass
Panicum virgatum	Switch-Grass, Panic Grass

Small Shrubs

Ardisia crenata	Coralberry
A. japonica	Japanese Ardisia, Marlberry
Gardenia augusta 'Radicans'	Dwarf Gardenia
Indigofera decora	Pink Indigo
Lagerstroemia hybrids	Dwarf Crepe Myrtles

Small to Medium Shrubs

Buddleia davidii	Butterfly Bush
Kerria japonica	Kerria, Japanese Kerria
Mahonia bealei	Leatherleaf Mahonia
M. fortunei	Chinese Mahonia

Medium to Large Shrubs

Abelia chinensis	Chinese Abelia
A. × 'Edward Goucher'	Edward Goucher Abelia
A. × *grandiflora*	Glossy Abelia

Plants That Need Regular Watering Until They Are Established (continued)

Medium to Large Shrubs (continued)

Callicarpa americana	American Beautyberry
C. bodinieri 'Profusion'	Bodinier Beautyberry
C. dichotoma	Purple Beautyberry
C. dichotoma 'Albifructus'	Purple Beautyberry 'Albifructus'
C. dichotoma 'Spring Gold'	Purple Beautyberry 'Spring Gold'
Illicium floridanum	Florida Anise-Tree
I. parviflorum	Small Anise-Tree

Plants That Are Drought-Tolerant

Medium to Large Shrubs

Viburnum suspensum	Sandankwa Viburnum

Large Shrubs and Small/Patio Trees

Ilex × attenuata 'East Palatka'	East Palatka Holly
I. × attenuata 'Fosters 2'	Foster Holly
I. × attenuata 'Humes'	Humes Holly
I. × attenuata 'Savannah'	Savannah Holly

Plants That Are Drought-Tolerant Once They Become Established

Medium to Large Shrubs

Bambusa multiplex	Clump Bamboo
Callistemon rigidus	Bottlebrush
Illicium parviflorum	Small Anise-Tree
Rhododendron prunifolium	Plumleaf Azalea
Stewartia monadelpha	Tall Stewartia
Viburnum awabuki	Awabuki Viburnum
Vitex angus-castus	Chaste Tree

Large Shrubs and Small/Patio Trees

Acer barbatum	Southern Sugar Maple, Florida Maple
A. leucoderme	Chalkbark Maple
Ilex × attenuata varieties	Holly
Koelreuteria bipinnata	Chinese Flame Tree
Ulmus parvifolia	Chinese Lacebark Elm

Plants That Need Well-Drained Soil

Ornamental Grasses

Chasmanthium latifolium	Wild Oats, Upland Sea Oats
Cymbopogon citratus	Lemon Grass
Imperata cylindrica rubra	Japanese Blood Grass
Liriope grandiflora	Evergreen Giant Liriope
L. muscari	Liriope

Plants That Need Well-Drained Soil (continued)

Ornamental Grasses (continued)

L. muscari 'Big Blue'	Big Blue Liriope
L. spicata	Creeping Lilyturf
Miscanthus spp.	Miscanthus
Muhlenbergia capillaris	Pink Muhly Sweetgrass
M. filipes	Purple Muhly Sweetgrass
Ophiopogon japonicus	Mondo Grass
O. japonicus 'Nana'	Dwarf Mondo Grass 'Nana'
Pennisetum alopecuroides	Fountain Grass
P. setaceum rubrum	Purple Fountain Grass

Annual Vines

Antigonon leptopus	Coral Vine
Aristolochia durior	Dutchman's Pipe
A. elegans	Calico Flower
Clerodendrum splendens	Bleeding Heart Vine
Clitoria ternatea 'Blue Sails'	Blue Sails Vine
Cobaea scandens	Cup-and-Saucer Vine
Dicentra scandens	Yellow Bleeding Heart Vine
Dolichos lablab Syn. *Lablab purpureus*	Hyacinth Bean
Ipomoea alba	Moonvine
I. × *multifida*	Cardinal Vine
I. tricolor	Morning Glory

Plants That Need Well-Drained Soil (continued)

Annual Vines (continued)

Mandevilla spp.	Mandevilla
Mascagnia macroptera	Yellow Orchid Vine, Butterfly Vine
Passiflora spp.	Passionflower
Phaseolus coccineus	Scarlet Runner Bean
Pseudogynoxys chenopodioides Syn. *Senecio confusus*	Mexican Flame Vine
Thunbergia alata	Black-Eyed Susan Vine
T. grandiflora	Blue Sky Vine, Blue Indian Vine
T. gregorii	Orange Clock Vine
Vigna (formerly *Phaseolus*) *caracalla*	Snail Vine, Caracalla Bean

Small Shrubs

Ardisia crenata	Coralberry
A. japonica	Japanese Ardisia, Marlberry
Gardenia augusta 'Radicans'	Dwarf Gardenia
Indigofera decora	Pink Indigo
Lagerstroemia hybrids	Dwarf Crepe Myrtles

Small to Medium Shrubs

Buddleia davidii	Butterfly Bush
Kerria japonica	Kerria, Japanese Kerria
Mahonia bealei	Leatherleaf Mahonia
M. fortunei	Chinese Mahonia

Plants That Need Well-Drained Soil (continued)

Medium to Large Shrubs

Abelia chinensis	Chinese Abelia
A. × 'Edward Goucher'	Edward Goucher Abelia
A. × grandiflora	Glossy Abelia
Callicarpa bodinieri 'Profusion'	Bodinier Beautyberry
C. dichotoma	Purple Beautyberry
C. dichotoma 'Albifructus'	Purple Beautyberry 'Albifructus'
C. 'Spring Gold'	Purple Beautyberry 'Spring Gold'
Callistemon rigidus	Bottlebrush
Hydrangea quercifolia	Oakleaf Hydrangea
Viburnum awabuki	Awabuki Viburnum
Vitex angus-castus	Chaste Tree

Large Shrubs and Small/Patio Trees

Acer leucoderme	Chalkbark Maple
Callistemon viminalis	Weeping Bottlebrush
× Citrofortunella mitis	Calamondin
Citrus limoni varieties	Meyer and Lisbon Lemon
Fortunella spp.	Kumquat
Ilex × attenuata 'East Palatka'	East Palatka Holly
I. × attenuata 'Fosters 2'	Foster Holly
I. × attenuata 'Humes'	Humes Holly
Koelreuteria bipinnata	Chinese Flame Tree
Magnolia grandiflora 'Little Gem'	Little Gem Magnolia

Plants That Prefer Rich, Well-Drained Soil

Medium to Large Shrubs

Hydrangea macrophylla macrophylla	Mophead Hydrangea
H. macrophylla normalis	Lacecap Hydrangea
Senna corymbosa formerly *Cassia corymbosa*	Flowery Senna
Stewartia monadelpha	Tall Stewartia

Plants That Prefer Well-Drained Soil with Moderate Fertility

Medium to Large Shrubs

Viburnum macrocephalum	Chinese Snowball Viburnum

Large Shrubs and Small/Patio Trees

Lagerstroemia spp.	Crepe Myrtles

Plants That Like Wet Sites

Ornamental Grasses

Andropogon glomeratus	Bushy Bluestem
Carex spp.	Sedge

Small Shrubs

Aronia melanocarpa	Black Chokeberry

Plants That Like Wet Sites (continued)

Small to Medium Shrubs

Clethra alnifolia	Clethra, Summersweet

Medium to Large Shrubs

Agarista populifolia or *Leucothoe populifolia*	Florida Leucothoe, Tall Leucothoe
Illicium floridanum	Florida Anise-Tree

Plants That Can Tolerate Wet Sites

Medium to Large Shrubs

Illicium parviflorum	Small Anise-Tree
Rhododendron serrulatum	Hammocksweet Azalea
R. viscosum	Swamp Azalea

Large Shrubs and Small/Patio Trees

Ilex × attenuata 'Savannah'	Savannah Holly

Plants That Are Tolerant of All Soil Types

Ornamental Grasses

Calamagrostis brachytricha	Korean Feather Reed Grass
Cortaderia selloana	Pampas Grass
Panicum virgatum	Switch-Grass, Panic Grass

Plants That Are Tolerant of All Soil Types (continued)
Medium to Large Shrubs

Illicium parviflorum	Small Anise-Tree

Plants That Prefer Dry, Sandy Soil
Medium to Large Shrubs

Viburnum suspensum	Sandankwa Viburnum

Plants That Don't Care about Soil Conditions
Medium to Large Shrubs

Callicarpa americana	American Beautyberry
Calycanthus floridus	Sweet Shrub, Carolina Allspice
Illicium floridanum	Florida Anise-Tree
I. parviflorum	Small Anise-Tree

Large Shrubs and Small/Patio Trees

Ulmus parvifolia	Chinese Lacebark Elm

Plants Arranged by Flower Color

Ornamental Grasses

Beige	*Miscanthus* spp.	Miscanthus
Blue-green	*Panicum virgatum*	Switch-Grass, Panic Grass
Lavender	*Liriope grandiflora*	Evergreen Giant Liriope
Lavender	*L. muscari*	Liriope
Lavender	*L. muscari* 'Big Blue'	Big Blue Liriope
Lavender	*L. spicata*	Creeping Lilyturf
Pink	*Muhlenbergia capillaris*	Pink Muhly Sweetgrass
Pink	*M. filipes*	Purple Muhly Sweetgrass
Purple	*Calamagrostis brachytricha*	Korean Feather Reed Grass
Purple	*Pennisetum setaceum rubrum*	Purple Fountain Grass
White	*Andropogon glomeratus*	Bushy Bluestem
White or pink	*Cortaderia selloana*	Pampas Grass
White to purple	*Pennisetum alopecuroides*	Fountain Grass

Annual Vines

Blue	*Clitoria ternatea*	'Blue Sails' Blue Sails Vine
Blue	*Thunbergia grandiflora*	Blue Sky Vine, Blue Indian Vine
Dark blue	*Cobaea scandens*	Cup-and-Saucer Vine
Deep lavender	*Dolichos lablab* Syn. *Lablab purpureus*	Hyacinth Bean
Mottled	*Aristolochia durior*	Dutchman's Pipe
Mottled	*A. elegans*	Calico Flower

Plants Arranged by Flower Color (continued)

Annual Vines (continued)

Orange	*Thunbergia gregorii*	Orange Clock Vine
Pink	*Antigonon leptopus*	Coral Vine
Red	*Ipomoea × multifida*	Cardinal Vine
Red	*Phaseolus coccineus*	Scarlet Runner Bean
Scarlet	*Clerodendrum splendens*	Bleeding Heart Vine
Vary	*Ipomoea tricolor*	Morning Glory
Vary	*Passiflora* spp.	Passionflower
White	*Ipomoea alba*	Moonvine
White or pink	*Mandevilla* spp.	Mandevilla
White to yellow	*Vigna* (formerly *Phaseolus*) *caracalla*	Snail Vine, Caracalla Bean
Yellow	*Dicentra scandens*	Yellow Bleeding Heart Vine
Yellow	*Mascagnia macroptera*	Yellow Orchid Vine, Butterfly Vine
Yellow	*Pseudogynoxys chenopodioides* Syn. *Senecio confusus*	Mexican Flame Vine
Yellow	*Thunbergia alata*	Blackeyed Susan Vine

Plants Arranged by Flower Color (continued)

Small Shrubs

Lavender pink	*Lagerstroemia* spp.	Crepe Myrtle 'Chickasaw'
Pink	*Ardisia japonica*	Japanese Ardisia, Marlberry
Pink	*Indigofera decora*	Pink Indigo
Rose pink	*Lagerstroemia* spp.	Crepe Myrtle 'Pocomoke'
White	*Gardenia augusta radicans*	Dwarf Gardenia
White to pink	*Ardisia crenata*	Coralberry

Small to Medium Shrubs

Lavender	*Lagerstroemia* spp.	Crepe Myrtle 'Ozark Spring'
Lavender to dark purple	*Buddleia davidii*	Butterfly Bush
Light red	*Lagerstroemia* spp.	Crepe Myrtle 'Firecracker'
Magenta	*Lagerstroemia* spp.	Crepe Myrtle 'Velma's Royal Delight'
Red	*Lagerstroemia* spp.	Crepe Myrtle 'Victor'
White, pink	*Clethra alnifolia*	Clethra, Summersweet
Yellow	*Kerria japonica*	Kerria, Japanese Kerria
Yellow	*Mahonia bealei*	Leatherleaf Mahonia
Yellow	*M. fortunei*	Chinese Mahonia

Plants Arranged by Flower Color (continued)

Medium to Large Shrubs

Blue	*Duranta erecta*	Golden Dewdrop, Sky Flower
Blue-pink*	Hydrangea *macrophylla* subsp. *macrophylla*	Mophead Hydrangea
Blue-pink*	*H. macrophylla* subsp. *macrophylla*	Mophead Hydrangea 'Nigra' aka 'Black Stem'
Dark pink	*Rhododendron viscosum*	Swamp Azalea 'Soir de Paris'
Greenish turning to white	*Viburnum macrocephalum*	Chinese Snowball Viburnum
Lilac to purple	*Vitex angus-castus*	Chaste Tree
Maroon	*Illicium floridanum*	Florida Anise-Tree 'Halley's Comet'
Orange-pink	*Rhododendron prunifolium*	Plumleaf Azalea 'Peach Glow'
Orange-red	*R. prunifolium*	Plumleaf Azalea
Pink	*Abelia* × 'Edward Goucher'	Edward Goucher Abelia
Pink	*Hydrangea macrophylla* subsp. *macrophylla*	Mophead Hydrangea 'Forever' Pink'
Pink	*H. macrophylla normalis*	Lacecap Hydrangea 'Geoffery Chadbud'
Pink	*Indigofera amblyantha*	no common name
Pink	*Loropetalum chinense* var. *rubrum*	Pink Flowering or Redleaf Loropetalum
Pink	*L. chinense* var. *rubrum*	Pink Flowering or Redleaf Loropetalum 'Zhuzhou Fuchsia'

* depending on pH

Plants Arranged by Flower Color (continued)

Medium to Large Shrubs (continued)

Pink	*Rhododendron viscosum*	Swamp Azalea 'Pink Rocket'
Pink	*Vitex angus-castus*	Chaste Tree 'Salina's Pink'
Pink-orange	*Rhododendron prunifolium*	Plumleaf Azalea 'Coral Glow'
Pink to white	*R. serrulatum*	Hammocksweet Azalea
Pink/golden blotches	*R. viscosum*	Swamp Azalea 'Jolie Madame'
Red	*Callistemon citrinus*	Lemon Bottlebrush
Red	*C. rigidus*	Stiff Bottlebrush
Red	*C. viminalis*	Weeping Bottlebrush ' Captain Cook'
Red	*C. viminalis*	Weeping Bottlebrush 'McCaskillii'
Red	*Calycanthus floridus*	Sweet Shrub, Carolina Allspice 'Edith Wilder'
Red	*Hydrangea macrophylla normalis*	Lacecap Hydrangea 'Kardinal Red'
Red	*Rhododendron prunifolium*	Plumleaf Azalea
Red (scarlet)	*R. prunifolium*	Plumleaf Azalea 'Lewis Shortt'
Red to wine	*Calycanthus floridus*	Sweet Shrub, Carolina Allspice
Red to wine	*C. floridus*	Sweet Shrub, Carolina Allspice 'Purpureus'

Plants Arranged by Flower Color (continued)

Medium to Large Shrubs (continued)

White	*Abelia chinensis*	Chinese Abelia
White	*A. × grandiflora*	Glossy Abelia
White	*Agarista populifolia* or *Leucothoe populifolia*	Tall Leucothoe, Florida Leucothoe
White	*Hydrangea macrophylla* subsp. *macrophylla*	Mophead Hydrangea 'Fuji Waterfall'
White	*H. macrophylla normalis* 'Larnarth White'	Lacecap Hydrangea
White turning to pink to tan	*H. quercifolia*	Oakleaf Hydrangea
White	*H. quercifolia*	Oakleaf Hydrangea 'Pee Wee'
White	*H. quercifolia*	Oakleaf Hydrangea 'Snowflake'
White turning to pink	*H. quercifolia*	Oakleaf Hydrangea 'Alice'
White turning to pink	*H. quercifolia*	Oakleaf Hydrangea 'Alison'
White turning to pink	*H. quercifolia*	Oakleaf Hydrangea 'Snow Queen'
White	*Illicium floridanum*	Florida Anise-Tree 'Semmes'
White with pink tinges	*Loropetalum chinense* var. *rubrum*	Pink Flowering or Redleaf Loropetalum 'Bicolor'

Plants Arranged by Flower Color (continued)

Medium to Large Shrubs (continued)

White	*Rhododendron viscosum*	Swamp Azalea
White	*Stewartia monadelpha*	Tall Stewartia
White	*Ternstroemia gymnanthera*	Japanese Ternstroemia, Cleyera
White	*Viburnum awabuki*	Awabuki Viburnum
White	*V. awabuki*	Awabuki Viburnum 'Chindo'
White	*V. suspensum*	Sandankwa Viburnum
Yellow	*Callistemon salignus*	Bottlebrush
Yellow	*Calycanthus floridus*	Sweet Shrub, Carolina Allspice 'Athens'
Yellow	*Rhododendron viscosum*	Swamp Azalea 'Arpege'
Yellow	*Senna corymbosa* formerly *Cassia corymbosa*	Flowery Senna
Yellow	*S. marilandica* formerly *C. marilandica*	Wild Senna

Plants Arranged by Flower Color (continued)

Large Shrubs and Small/Patio Trees

Bright pink	*Lagerstroemia* spp.	Crepe Myrtle 'Choctaw'
Bright pink	*Lagerstroemia* spp.	Crepe Myrtle 'Royal Velvet'
Bright red	*Lagerstroemia* spp.	Crepe Myrtle 'Red Rocket'
Coral pink	*Lagerstroemia* spp.	Crepe Myrtle 'Comanche'
Dark coral pink	*Lagerstroemia* spp.	Crepe Myrtle 'Miami'
Dark coral pink	*Lagerstroemia* spp.	Crepe Myrtle 'Tuscarora'
Dark pink	*Lagerstroemia* spp.	Crepe Myrtle 'Sioux'
Dark pink	*Lagerstroemia* spp.	Crepe Myrtle 'Tuskegee'
Dark pink	*Lagerstroemia* spp.	Crepe Myrtle 'William Toovey'
Dark red	*Lagerstroemia* spp.	Crepe Myrtle 'Byer's Regal Red'
Deep red	*Lagerstroemia* spp.	Crepe Myrtle 'Dynamite'
Electric red	*Lagerstroemia* spp.	Crepe Myrtle 'Centennial Spirit'
Lavender	*Lagerstroemia* spp.	Crepe Myrtle 'Byer's Hardy Lavender'
Lavender	*Lagerstroemia* spp.	Crepe Myrtle 'Conestoga'
Lavender	*Lagerstroemia* spp.	Crepe Myrtle 'Lipan'
Lavender	*Lagerstroemia* spp.	Crepe Myrtle 'Powhatan'
Lavender	*Lagerstroemia* spp.	Crepe Myrtle 'Wichita'
Lavender	*Lagerstroemia* spp.	Crepe Myrtle 'Yuma'

Plants Arranged by Flower Color (continued)

Large Shrubs and Small/Patio Trees (continued)

Lavender pink	*Lagerstroemia* spp.	Crepe Myrtle 'Basham's Party Pink'
Light lavender	*Lagerstroemia* spp.	Crepe Myrtle 'Apalachee'
Light lavender	*Lagerstroemia* spp.	Crepe Myrtle 'Muskogee'
Light pink	*Lagerstroemia* spp.	Crepe Myrtle 'Osage'
Medium pink	*Lagerstroemia* spp.	Crepe Myrtle 'Potomac'
Medium pink	*Lagerstroemia* spp.	Crepe Myrtle 'Seminole'
Pale pink	*Lagerstroemia* spp.	Crepe Myrtle 'Biloxi'
Purple	*Lagerstroemia* spp.	Crepe Myrtle 'Catawba'
Red	*Callistemon viminalis*	Weeping Bottlebrush
Red	*C. viminalis*	Weeping Bottlebrush 'Red Cascade'
Red	*Lagerstroemia* spp.	Crepe Myrtle 'Country Red'
Red	*Lagerstroemia* spp.	Crepe Myrtle 'Dallas Red'
Red with white edges	*Lagerstroemia* spp.	Crepe Myrtle 'Raspberry Sundae'
White	× *Citrofortunella mitis*	Calamondin
White	*Citrus limoni* varieties	Meyer and Lisbon Lemon
White	*Fortunella* spp.	Kumquat
White	*Ilex* × *attenuata* 'East Palatka'	East Palatka Holly
White	*I.* × *attenuata* 'Fosters 2'	Foster Holly
White	*I.* × *attenuata* 'Humes'	Humes Holly
White	*I.* × *attenuata* 'Savannah'	Savannah Holly

Plants Arranged by Flower Color (continued)

Large Shrubs and Small/Patio Trees (continued)

White	*Lagerstroemia* spp.	Crepe Myrtle 'Byer's Wonderful White'
White	*Lagerstroemia* spp.	Crepe Myrtle 'Fantasy'
White	*Lagerstroemia* spp.	Crepe Myrtle 'Kiowa'
White	*Lagerstroemia fauriei*	Crepe Myrtle 'Fauriei'
White	*Lagerstroemia* spp.	Crepe Myrtle 'Natchez'
White	*Lagerstroemia* spp.	Crepe Myrtle 'Sarah's Favorite'
White	*Lagerstroemia* spp.	Crepe Myrtle 'Townhouse'
White	*Magnolia grandiflora*	Little Gem Magnolia 'Little Gem'
White	*Ulmus parvifolia*	Chinese Lacebark Elm
Yellow	*Koelreuteria bipinnata*	Chinese Flame Tree

Plants Chosen for Berry/Seed/Fruit Color

Ornamental Grasses

Beige	*Cortaderia selloana*	Pampas Grass
Black	*Liriope grandiflora*	Evergreen Giant Liriope
Black	*L. muscari*	Liriope
Black	*L. muscari* 'Big Blue'	Big Blue Liriope
Black	*L. spicata*	Creeping Lilyturf
Bronze	*Andropogon glomeratus*	Bushy Bluestem

Plants Chosen for Berry/Seed/Fruit Color (continued)

Ornamental Grasses (continued)

Bronze	*Chasmanthium latifolium*	Wild Oats, Upland Sea Oats
Bronze	*Pennisetum setaceum rubrum*	Purple Fountain Grass
Light brown	*Miscanthus* spp.	Miscanthus
Silver gray	*Calamagrostis brachytricha*	Korean Feather Reed Grass
White/beige	*Pennisetum alopecuroides*	Fountain Grass

Annual Vines

Brown	*Ipomoea alba*	Moonvine
Chartreuse	*Mascagnia macroptera*	Yellow Orchid Vine, Butterfly Vine
Green	*Phaseolus coccineus*	Scarlet Runner Bean
Purple	*Dolichos lablab* Syn. *Lablab purpureus*	Hyacinth Bean

Small Shrubs

Black	*Aronia melanocarpa*	Black Chokeberry
Brown	*Lagerstroemia* hybrids	Dwarf Crepe Myrtles
Red	*Ardisia crenata*	Coralberry
Red	*A. japonica*	Japanese Ardisia, Marlberry

Plants Chosen for Berry/Seed/Fruit Color (continued)

Small to Medium Shrubs

Black	*Buddleia davidii*	Butterfly Bush
Gray blue	*Mahonia bealei*	Leatherleaf Mahonia
Light green	*Clethra alnifolia*	Clethra, Summersweet

Medium to Large Shrubs

Black	*Callicarpa acuminata*	Mexican Beautyberry
Lavender to purple	*C. dichotoma*	Purple Beautyberry
Light brown	*Illicium floridanum*	Florida Anise-Tree
Pink to lavender	*Callicarpa bodinieri* 'Profusion'	Bodinier Beautyberry 'Profusion'
Purple	*C. dichotoma*	Purple Beautyberry 'Spring Gold'
Raspberry red	*C. acuminata* 'Woodlanders'	Mexican Beautyberry 'Woodlanders'
Red	*Viburnum awabuki*	Awabuki Viburnum
Red	*V. awabuki* 'Chindo'	Awabuki Viburnum 'Chindo'
Red turning black	*V. suspensum*	Sandankwa Viburnum
Violet to magenta	*Callicarpa americana*	American Beautyberry

Plants Chosen for Berry/Seed/Fruit Color (continued)

Medium to Large Shrubs (continued)

White	*C. dichotoma* 'Albifructus'	Purple Beautyberry 'Albifructus'
Yellow	*Duranta erecta*	Golden Dewdrop, Sky Flower

Large Shrubs and Small/Patio Trees

Green turning orange	× *Citrofortunella mitis*	Calamondin
Green turning orange	*Fortunella* spp.	Kumquat
Green turning yellow	*Citrus limoni* varieties	Meyer and Lisbon Lemon
Light green	*Ulmus parvifolia*	Chinese Lacebark Elm
Pink seedpods	*Koelreuteria bipinnata*	Chinese Flame Tree
Red	*Ilex* × *attenuata* 'East Palatka'	East Palatka Holly
Red	*I.* × *attenuata* 'Fosters 2'	Foster Holly
Red	*I.* × *attenuata* 'Humes'	Humes Holly
Red	*I.* × *attenuata* 'Savannah'	Savannah Holly
Red	*Magnolia grandiflora*	Little Gem Magnolia 'Little Gem'

Plants with Interesting Bark

Small to Medium Shrubs

Gray-brown	*Lagerstroemia* spp.	Crepe Myrtle 'Ozark Spring'
Green stems in summer; yellow stems in fall	*Kerria japonica*	Kerria, Japanese Kerria
Light gray	*Lagerstroemia* spp.	Crepe Myrtle 'Velma's Royal Delight'

Medium to Large Shrubs

Cinnamon	*Stewartia monadelpha*	Tall Stewartia
Exfoliates	*Abelia chinensis*	Chinese Abelia
Exfoliates to cinnamon brown	*Hydrangea quercifolia*	Oakleaf Hydrangea

Large Shrubs and Small/Patio Trees

See Crepe Myrtle Varieties chart pp. 154-157	*Lagerstroemia* spp.	Crepe Myrtle
Brown, gray, green, and orange lacy pattern	*Ulmus parvifolia*	Chinese Lacebark Elm

Plants with Interesting Leaf Color

Ornamental Grasses

Bronze in fall	*Andropogon glomeratus*	Bushy Blue Stem
Bronze to beige depending on species	*Carex* spp.	Sedge
Purple (new blades)	*Pennisetum setaceum* 'Rubrum'	Purple Fountain Grass
Red	*Imperata cylindrica* 'Rubra'	Japanese Blood Grass

Annual Vines

Lavender	*Dolichos lablab* Syn. *Lablab purpureus*	Hyacinth Bean

Medium to Large Shrubs

Black maroon	*Loropetalum chinense* var. *rubrum* 'Zhuzhou Fushsia'	Pink Flowering or Redleaf Loropetalum
Black to dark purple stems	*Hydrangea macrophylla* subsp. *macrophylla* 'Nigra' aka 'Black Stem'	Mophead Hydrangea
Burgundy-red in fall	*H. quercifolia* 'Alice'	Oakleaf Hydrangea
Burgundy-red in fall	*H. quercifolia* 'Alison'	Oakleaf Hydrangea
Gold turning to green	*Callicarpa dichotoma*	Purple Beautyberry 'Spring Gold'

Plants with Interesting Leaf Color (continued)

Medium to Large Shrubs (continued)

Maroon	*Hydrangea quercifolia*	Oakleaf Hydrangea 'Snowflake'
Purple	*Calycanthus floridus* 'Purpureus'	Sweet Shrub, Carolina Allspice
Purple	*Loropetalum chinense* var. *rubrum*	Pink Flowering or Redleaf Loropetalum
Purple	*L. chinense* var. *rubrum* 'Bicolor'	Pink Flowering or Redleaf Loropetalum
Reddish tint in spring	*Agarista populifolia* or *Leucothoe populifolia*	Florida Leucothoe, Tall Leucothoe
Red, orange, or purple in fall depending on variety	*Hydrangea quercifolia*	Oakleaf Hydrangea
Red-purple in fall	*H. quercifolia* 'Pee Wee'	Oakleaf Hydrangea
Red-bronze in fall	*H. quercifolia* 'Snow Queen'	Oakleaf Hydrangea
Red to maroon in fall	*Stewartia monadelpha*	Tall Stewartia
Red turning glossy green	*Ternstroemia gymnanthera* Cleyera	Japanese Ternstroemia,
Yellow/golden	*Kerria japonica*	Kerria, Japanese Kerria

Plants with Interesting Leaf Color (continued)

Large Shrubs and Small/Patio Trees

Yellow to orange in fall	*Acer barbatum*	Southern Sugar Maple, Florida Maple
Yellow, orange, red in fall	*A. leucoderme*	Chalkbark Maple

Fragrant Plants

Ornamental Grasses

Cymbopogon citratus	Lemon Grass	Pleasant

Annual Vines

Aristolochia durior	Dutchman's Pipe	Unpleasant
Dolichos lablab Syn. *Lablab purpureus*	Hyacinth Bean	Slight
Ipomoea alba	Moonvine	Pleasant
Mandevilla laxa	Chilean Jasmine	Pleasant
Passiflora × 'Elizabeth'	Passionflower	Pleasant
P. × 'Incense'	Passionflower	Pleasant
Vigna (formerly *Phaseolus*) *caracalla*	Snail Vine, Caracalla Bean	Pleasant

Small Shrubs

Gardenia augusta 'Radicans'	Drawf Gardenia	Pleasant
Indigofera decora	Pink Indigo	Pleasant

Fragrant Plants (continued)

Small to Medium Shrubs

Buddleia davidii	Butterfly Bush	Pleasant
Clethra alnifolia	Clethra, Summersweet	Pleasant
Mahonia fortunei	Chinese Mahonia	Pleasant

Medium to Large Shrubs

Abelia chinensis	Chinese Abelia	Pleasant
Agarista populifolia or *Leucothoe populifolia*	Florida Leucothoe, Tall Leucothoe	Pleasant
Callistemon citrinus	Lemon Bottlebrush	Pleasant
C. rigidus	Stiff Bottlebrush	Pungent
Calycanthus floridus	Sweet Shrub, Carolina Allspice	Pleasant
C. floridus	Sweet Shrub, Carolina Allspice 'Athens'	Pleasant
C. floridus	Sweet Shrub, Carolina Allspice 'Edith Wilder'	Pleasant
Illicium floridanum	Florida Anise-Tree	Pungent flower
I. parviflorum	Anise-Tree	Pleasant
Rhododendron serrulatum	Hammocksweet Azalea	Pleasant
R. viscosum	Swamp Azalea	Pleasant
R. viscosum	Swamp Azalea 'Arpege'	Pleasant
R. viscosum	Swamp Azalea 'Jolie Madame'	Pleasant

Fragrant Plants (continued)

Medium to Large Shrubs (continued)

R. viscosum	Swamp Azalea 'Pink Rocket'	Pleasant
R. viscosum	Swamp Azalea 'Soir de Paris'	Pleasant
Stewartia monadelpha	Tall Stewartia	Pleasant

Large Shrubs and Small/Patio Trees

Fortunella spp.	Kumquat	Pleasant
× Citrofortunella mitis	Calamondin	Pleasant
Citrus limoni varieties	Meyer and Lisbon Lemon	Pleasant
Magnolia grandiflora 'Little Gem'	Little Gem Magnolia	Pleasant

Plants That Survive Heat and Humidity but Have No Significant Summertime Ornamental Value

Although the following plants did not meet our *Some Like It Hot* criteria for offering robust bloom, vibrant berries, interesting bark, or, at the very least, exceptional leaf color during the summer months, they still have merit. Perhaps they could be described as the strong, silent type. They patiently survive the deep south's annual steam bath while not making demands on their keepers. Many of them are old friends and they certainly deserve recognition.

Aucuba japonica	Aucuba
Berberis spp.	Barberry
Camellia spp.	Camellia
Chaenomeles spp.	Quince
Chionanthus retusus	Chinese Fringetree
C. virginicus	Fringetree
Cycas revoluta	Sago Palm
Deutzia spp.	Deutzia
Eriobotrya japonica	Loquat
Euonymus spp.	Euonymus
Fatsia japonica	Fatsia
Feijoa sellowiana	Pineapple Guava
Ilex crenata	Japanese Hollies
I. latifolia	Lusterleaf Holly
I. vomitoria	Yaupon Holly
I. vomitoria nana	Dwarf Yaupon Holly

Plants That Survive Heat and Humidity but Have No Significant Summertime Ornamental Value (continued)

I. vomitoria pendula	Weeping Yaupon Holly
Itea japonica	Japanese Sweetspire
I. virginica	Virginia Sweetspire
Ligustrum spp.	Privet
Myrica cerifera	Wax Myrtle
Nandina domestica	Heavenly Bamboo
Oleander nerium	Oleander
Philadelphus spp.	Mock Orange
Pieris japonica	Japanese Pieris
Pittosporum spp.	Pittosporum
Podocarpus macrophyllus	Podocarpus
Punica granatum	Pomegranate
Pyracantha spp.	Pyracantha
Sabal minor	Dwarf Palmetto Palm
Spirea spp.	Spireas
Viburnum dentatum	Arrowwood Viburnum
V. japonica	Japanese Viburnum
V. obovatum	Small Viburnum
V. prunifolium	Blackhaw Viburnum
Yucca spp.	Yucca

Suppliers
of Plants

One of the frustrating things about gardening is getting all worked up over a new discovery and then not finding the plant at your local garden center. We know that for the intrepid plant fanatic the hunting is half the fun, but we also recognize that some of the flora discussed in *Some Like It Hot* may not be easy to locate. We have, therefore, included a list of suppliers who carry some of the plants we have mentioned.

We offer both retail and wholesale establishments, as well as a few seed companies for growers. It has been our experience that gardening establishments are usually quite willing to oblige customer requests. Supplying them with the name and address of a wholesaler who carries a particular plant speeds up the ordering process. Of course, many gardeners have discovered the fun of purchasing plants themselves from mail-order businesses. There's nothing better than receiving shiny little plants snuggled in a box on a dank winter's day.

Retail Mail Order – Plants

Noble Plants
337 S. Milledge Ave., Suite 125
Athens, GA 30605
Tel. and fax: 706-613-0046
www.nobleplants.com

Nurseries Carolinana (*also wholesale*)
22 Stephens Estate
North Augusta, SC 29860
803-279-2707
www.nurcar.com

Stokes Tropical
4806 E. Old Spanish Trail
Jeanerette, LA 70544
Orders: 800-624-9706
Information: 337-365-6998
Fax: 337-365-6991
www.stokestropicals.com

Woodlanders
1128 Colleton Ave.
Aiken, SC 29801
803-648-7522
www.woodlanders.net

Yucca Do Nursery
P.O. Box 907
Hempstead, TX 77445
979-826-4580
Fax 979-826-4571
www.yuccado.com

Retail Mail Order – Seeds

W. Atlee Burpee & Co.
Warminster, PA 18974
800-888-1447
Fax 800-487-5530
www.burpee.com

Geo. W. Park Seed® Co., Inc.
1 Parkton Ave.
Greenwood, SC 29647-0001
800-845-3369
Fax 800-275-9941
www.parkseed.com

Thompson & Morgan Seedsmen, Inc.
P.O. Box 1308
Jackson, NH 08527-0308
800-274-7333
Fax 888-466-4769
www.thompson-morgan.com

Whatcom Seed Company
P.O. Box 40700
Eugene, OR 97404
www.seedrack.com

Wholesale – Plants

Sandy Hill Plant Farm
P.O. Box 329
Mineola, TX 75773
sandyhillplantfarm@earthlink.net
www.sandyhillplantfarm.com

San Felasco
7315 N.W. 126th St.
Gainesville, FL 32653
352-332-1220
www.sanfelasco.com

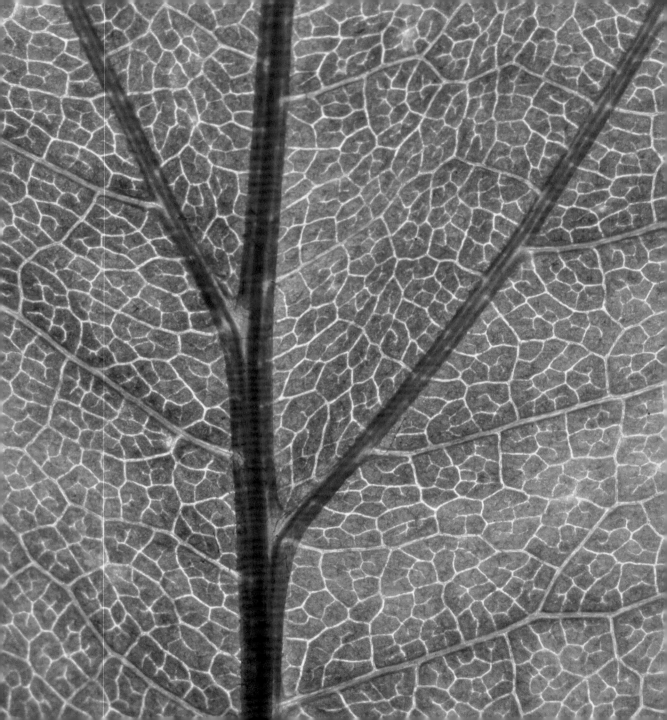

Recommended Reading

We are often asked about our personal gardening book preferences. That's a difficult question to answer because we're nuts about practically every gardening book we can get our hands on. However, the following is our collective list of workhorse, can't-live-without books. These are the friends that we immediately turn to when we need dependable horticultural information.

Adams, William D. and Thomas R. Leroy. *Growing Fruits and Nuts in the South: The Definitive Guide.* Dallas: Taylor Publishing Company, 1992.

Armitage, Allan. *Armitage's Manual of Annuals, Biennials, and Half-Hardy Perennials.* Portland, OR: Timber Press, 2001.

Barash, Cathy Wilkinson. *The Climbing Garden.* New York: Friedman/ Fairfax Publishers, 2000.

Crandall, Chuck and Barbara Crandall. *Flowering, Fruiting & Foliage Vines: A Gardener's Guide.* New York: Sterling Publishing Company, Inc., 1995.

Darke, Rick. *Color Encyclopedia of Ornamental Grasses.* Portland, OR: Timber Press, 1999.

Dirr, Michael. *Manual of Woody Landscape Plants: Their Identification, Ornamental Characteristics, Culture, Propagation and Uses.* 5th ed. Champaign, IL: Stipes Publishing, 1998.

Dirr, Michael. *Dirr's Hardy Trees and Shrubs: An Illustrated Encyclopedia.* Portland, OR: Timber Press, 1997.

Dirr, Michael. *Dirr's Trees and Shrubs for Warm Climates: An Illustrated Encyclopedia.* Portland, OR: Timber Press, 2002.

Dirr, Michael and Charles W. Heuser, Jr. *The Reference Manual of Woody Plant Propagation: From Seed to Tissue Culture: A Practical Working Guide to the Propagation of Over 1100 Species, Varieties, and Cultivars.* Athens, GA: Varsity Press, 1987.

Foote, Leonard E. and Samuel B. Jones, Jr. *Native Shrubs and Woody Vines of the Southeast*. Portland, OR: Timber Press, 1998.

Galle, Fred C. *Azaleas*. Portland, OR: Timber Press, 1987.

Galle, Fred C. *Hollies: The Genus Ilex*. Portland, OR: Timber Press, 1997.

Greenlee, John. *The Encyclopedia of Ornamental Grasses*. Emmaus, PA: Rodale Press, 1992.

Grounds, Roger. *The Plantfinder's Guide to Ornamental Grasses*. Portland, OR: Timber Press, 1998.

Jefferson-Brown, Michael. *Ramblers Scramblers & Twiners: High-performance Climbing Plants & Wall Shrubs*. UK: David & Charles Brunel House, 1999.

Klein, Maggie, Paul Moore and Claude Sweet. *All About Citrus & Subtropical Fruits*. Ed. Rick Bond. San Francisco: Ortho Books, 1985.

Vanderplank, John. *Passion Flowers*. 3rd ed. Cambridge, MA: MIT Press, 2000.

Wyman, Donald. *Wyman's Gardening Encyclopedia*. New York: Scribner, 1986.

Index

All photographs by F. Brian Smith, except
p. 42 Terry Forsyth
p. 50 Pam Subjek
p. 72 U.S. Geological Survey /
photo by Forest and Kim Starr
p. 111 Richard Dwight Porcher

Front cover: Yellow Bleeding Heart Vine
(*Dicentra scandens*)